Talking Turkey
the language, culture and identity of
Turkish speaking children in Britain

Talking Turkey
the language, culture and identity of Turkish speaking children in Britain

Tözün Issa

Trentham Books
Stoke on Trent, UK and Sterling, USA

Trentham Books Limited

Westview House	22883 Quicksilver Drive
734 London Road	Sterling
Oakhill	VA 20166-2012
Stoke on Trent	USA
Staffordshire	
England ST4 5NP	

© 2005 Tözün Issa

First published 2005

British Library Cataloguing-in-Publication Data
A catalogue record for this book is available from the British Library

ISBN-13: 978-1-85856-318-3
ISBN-10: 1-85856-318-6

Designed and typeset by Trentham Print Design Ltd, Chester and printed in Great Britain by Cromwell Press Ltd., Wiltshire.

Contents

Acknowledgements

I would like to thank my supervisors Alistair Ross and Alan Newland for their invaluable advice and patience while I undertook this research. I am also grateful to Cathy Pomphrey, Pat East, Jill Rutter for their valuable comments on various sections of this book. I thank Frances Vickers for reading and picking out intricate but equally important details.

While researching this book, I was fortunate to share the expertise of a number of professionals from the Kurdish community in London. I would especially like to thank Yashar Ismailoğlu and Fesih Eren for their contributions.

I had the opportunity to visit a number of schools and talked to many teachers about their bilingual practices. I would especially like to thank Kelami Dedezade, Varinder Bakshi and Simran Dhillon for allowing me into their classrooms and for sharing their expertise.

I would like to thank year 6 children and their teacher Caroline O'Sullivan from Stewart Headlam school for cover drawings, also Gillian Klein for her expert advice, but most of all for having faith in me. I thank my family for their support and encouragement and finally MSCS enterprises for inspiration and energy.

Foreword

Tözün Issa offers us a book that is both timely and important. The Turkish and Cypriot communities have been part of British life for over a century, and have settled in Britain in significant numbers for over forty years. Cyprus is now a member of the European Union. Turkey is on the verge of being accepted as a candidate country for EU membership, which should mean that within a decade all Turkish citizens will enjoy the same full residence, working and civil rights in Britain that Irish, French and Cypriots already have. People of Turkish origin, whether from Cyprus, Turkey or the Turkish diaspora contribute in a significant way to contemporary society in Britain, and this book helps us both mark and welcome that contribution, and deepens our understanding of how the children of Turkish origin make their way in Britain today.

This book sets the context of the patterns of Turkish and Cypriot settlement and participation in British towns and cities, tracing the economic, political and social factors linked to this. This useful analysis sets the context for Tözün Issa's main thrust: how do these factors help us understand the language, culture and identity of Turkish-speaking children? His empirical data, gathered from hours of conversation and interaction with primary school-aged children, in both Turkish and English, reveals a wealth of detail about how these second and third generation young Britons construct cultural and social identities around the economies and practices of their parents and relatives. Set in the economic context of the generally small-scale trader, entrepreneur and importer, these children use their knowledge, observations of domestic life and business, and experience, to build wider understandings of the social world, supported by particular elements of each of their languages. Tozun's particular contribution is to illuminate the detailed contributions that each language makes to this development of social understanding, and how subtly different concepts are drawn from each culture and synthesised to create a view of the world.

Focusing on a small range of economic concepts in this way allows the reader to follow the intricacies of how familial and cultural patterns of behaviour contribute in a very particular way to the development of culturally related concepts – in particular, work, cost, money and trading. He sets the development of bilingual identities within the current English national curriculum, and in particular the emphasis on English, rather than language, and the consequent status – or lack of status – given to community languages in many schools. Tözün suggest useful ways in which teachers can overcome their apprehensions about using languages other than English in the classroom, and provides positive models of bilingual teaching. In particular, he identifies using culturally relevant resources, including the use of familiar settings and roles that allow identification and provide focus.

This book has its primary focus on the Turkish-speaking communities. The detail with which Tözün unpicks the oversimplistic notion of 'Turkish' is of special value in this respect. He shows how this portmanteau term is used to mask a whole range of different identities, cultural and linguistic groups. He identifies and addresses the particularities of the Kurdish people, who all too frequently included in the term 'Turkish'. The differences between mainland Turkish communities and Cypriot Turkish communities is explored, in terms of their language, cultural and social patterns and relative status.

This same sensitivity shows in his approaches to individual differences between the children whose language and activities he analyses. Informal collaborative activities can be used in the classroom to enable children to speak both their languages more freely. Tözün shows how these bilinguals seem to rely on one of their languages to transfer vocabulary and meaning in a particular conceptual area: the interplay and interrelationship between the two languages gives a richer understanding and depth to the ideas in both languages. And the ideas themselves are much more elaborate than might have been suspected by the causal adult observer: the notions focused on here – of economic behaviour around price, work and money – show that these children have a complexity and elaboration in their understanding far beyond any simple definition.

But the appeal and value of this book is to a much wider group than simply educators working with communities of Turkish origin. There is a much wider debate on education within diverse society that relates to both the specific provisions that may be needed for a minority group (ethnic, linguistic or other) and to the need to simultaneously address the learning of all children about the value – and values – of a diverse society. This book makes valuable contributions to this area.

Alistair Ross
Director, Institute for Policy Studies in Education
London Metropolitan University

Introduction

This book explores how children's cultural experiences affect their learning. The word culture has a variety of understandings attached to its meaning. Ross (2003) articulates this well when he concludes that its different interpretations are '..not neutral'. (p 3), 'socially constructed' and are determined by 'the environment rather than the genes' (p 4). All these processes are dynamic and constantly changing. This book takes account of the dynamics of such change, exploring the cultural practices of linguistic communities and the ways these affect the acquisition of related concepts. The topic of study in this book relates to one linguistic group: Turkish speaking communities in the UK.

I examine children's understanding of culturally related concepts such as cost, money, buying and work. I investigate through practical activities how children' understanding about these matters can develop further through organised role-playing contexts which present areas of new learning as challenges. Consequently the activities presented in part 2 assist the process of development through a series of interrelated tasks for the children. I discovered, however, that not all children follow the same processes of development in each of these areas and these findings are also discussed.

The education of the Turkish speaking communities has been a preoccupation of educators, community activists and classroom teachers for over half a century, ever since the first generation of Cypriot pupils arrived in British schools. Since then, there have been numerous studies both local and national to assess the factors contributing to their underachievement. Although there are emerging trends of recognisable improvement in some local education authorities (LEAs), the statistical information indicates levels which are still below national standards.

The debate surrounding the 'remedies' for tackling underachievement by Turkish speaking pupils is complex. It is influenced by a variety of factors. The first relates to lack of knowledge about several different communities which until recently were lumped together by most LEAs under the category 'Turkish speaking'. For the Kurdish speaking community in particular this raises an issue of identity. Many Kurdish educators to whom I spoke about this book have rightly objected to being placed in such a broad category, on political and historical grounds that concern the status of Kurdish as a language of national identity. As a researcher this was an important dimension to consider and underline before embarking on such a project. Equally, the teaching and use of Kurdish as a language in schools is an issue to be explored.

For Cypriot Turkish speakers there is also an issue of identity, reflected in the use of a Cypriot variety of Turkish. The present practices both within the mainstream – what little mainstream provision of Turkish there is – and supplementary schools are cause for concern. The emotional and psychological effects of not having opportunities to use one's own variety of Turkish is an issue explored in the context of the activities set out in the book. This also applies to other regional variations of Turkish which more accurately represent the Turkish speaking school population in London schools. These are issues which present particular challenges for the communities and need urgent attention.

The second factor concerns practice in mainstream schools. Since the introduction of the national curriculum we have seen that policies adhering to national standards have failed to address the issues facing these linguistic communities. There is little doubt that in the present educational climate emphasising *English* rather than *language* development does not help the debate for bilingual models of teaching. There may be widespread support within governmental organisations for promoting the use of children's community languages but there is a glaring lack of practical examples of how this could be incorporated into the existing prescribed structures within classrooms. Teachers clearly need training to acquire skills for facilitating the use and development of children's first languages in classrooms. Partly, they need to overcome their anxiety about using another language in addition to English in their classrooms.

Teachers need positive models of bilingual teaching to use and experiment with in lessons. The teaching approaches explored in this book are intended to help provide them.

The activities presented here are chosen as models for classroom practice for all pupils but offer particular emphasis and strength in meeting the needs of bilingual pupils. They are planned specifically to promote:

■ Children's use and development of oracy: giving opportunities to children to express themselves through different channels of communication, using language/s familiar to them and creating opportunities to listen to and debate the views of others around them. The underlying principle is to explore the processes of thinking through different linguistic tools, which eventually lead to new areas of learning.

■ Collaboration, through 'challenged' groups: creating an interactive talking and listening group, that is given specific task/s to question, debate and resolve to meet a challenge set by the teacher. Children listen to others, share their own views with others and eventually inform their own thinking in relation to existing information. This facilitates the use of both languages in a meaningful context.

■ Differentiation though the use of culturally relevant resources: This is the key focus for most teachers working with bilingual children. The type of material used in lessons is designed to be familiar, interactive and visual so as to encourage all the children in the class to take part.

All three strategies need to be perceived in the context of well-planned lessons that have clear learning outcomes and structures for delivery.

The book is in two parts. In the first part, Chapter 1 looks at each Turkish speaking community in some detail and explores the patterns of migration and settlement into Britain.

Chapter 2 explores the issues of language and identity. It looks at key factors affecting the communities and discusses the key differences and similarities in how each uses Turkish. It indicates important aspects of the Kurdish language and its key role in maintaining identity.

Chapter 3 explores the role of language within community based activities, family life and structure and the employment patterns of Turkish speakers in the UK. The importance is stressed of community-based activities in maintaining the use of Turkish and Kurdish and how they foster understanding of economic concepts.

Part 2 focuses on language use in informal role-play settings. It explores children's use of economic concepts when they play shop. Turkish speaking children often encounter such concepts at a young age. They help in their parents' shops, observing the interaction between their parents as shopkeepers and customers. They have the chance to explore the relationship between buying and selling, how profit is made and they see that money is an important commodity in exchange for work undertaken. Through these processes children develop their understanding of concepts such as cost, money, buying and work. Chapters 4, 5, 6 and 7 examine how these concepts develop.

In Chapter 8, I present three examples of bilingual classroom practice in primary and secondary contexts. The first, from a science lesson in Turkish/English, explores the ways children's knowledge about their natural environment can be used to further their learning. The teacher's use of the two languages is considered in the context of the specific learning outcomes.

The second example is a Maths lesson in a Panjabi state funded secondary school in Hayes. I pay particular attention to the teacher's use of a variety of visual resources to maintain children's interest. It is an example of how a maths activity can be made fun through interactive strategies in two languages.

The third activity is from another Panjabi school, this time a primary school in Essex. The class teacher and I wanted to develop the shop transaction processes explored with the Turkish children further. The children's collaborative skills are explored through a series of challenges concerning the prices of items sold in a shop. The children's own experience of bargaining in Panjabi shops is used as basis for setting up and organising appropriate challenges for this activity.

The main concern of this book is to throw new light on how bilingual children learn. The ideas and practical examples presented suggest that just as there are common approaches to teaching bilingual children there are also specific aspects relating to their own cultural experiences that make the process virtually unique for each pupil.

The ideas explored in this book are based on my own research and classroom practice as well as my observations of colleagues in supplementary and mainstream schools. So one reason for writing the book is that I wish to share my experiences with colleagues who are involved with the education of Turkish speaking children.

A second reason follows on from the first. The book is intended to contribute to the current debate on the education of ethnic minority communities generally and Turkish speaking communities specifically. The issue of underachievement is a complex one and needs to be explored from a multiplicity of perspectives, which are intrinsically connected: the classroom, the school and the wider school community. What I try and do in this book is to explore some of the specific cultural experiences of the Turkish speaking communities and present possible ways these could be used as in the everyday activities of classrooms.

Part 1

Turkish Speaking Communities in Britain: migration, identity and economic activities

1

Migration and settlement

The Turkish Speaking population in Britain is not homogenous. It is made up of three distinct groups: Turkish-speaking Cypriots, Turks from mainland Turkey and Turkish-speaking Kurds, also from mainland Turkey. There are also a small numbers of Turkish speaking Kurds and Roma/ Gypsy refugees who arrived from Cyprus during the mid-1990s. It is estimated that the overall population of Turkish speakers in the UK is around 180,000-200,000 (Mehmet Ali, 2001). In this chapter I discuss each group in terms of migration and settlement patterns.

Turkish Cypriots

There are varying estimations of the population of the Turkish speaking communities in Britain. Earliest data appear only to refer to the 'Cypriot born' population. Table 1 gives us the number of Cypriots resident in Britain, male and female, Turkish and Greek speaking, residing in Britain between 1951and1981.

Turkish speaking communities in Britain vary markedly in size. Oakley (1970) has calculated a Cypriot population of 110,000 and estimated it to have reached around 140,000 in 1977 (Constantinides, 1977; and Triseliotis, 1976) put the figure as high as 160,000. The census data does not distinguish between Turkish and Greek Cypriots. The ratio of the population in the UK is similar to that of Cyprus – approximately 1:5 Turkish to Greek Cypriots. Reid *et al* (1985) estimated that there were 7000 Turkish speakers living in London borough of Haringey alone. In 1986 the

Table 1: Cypriot-born population resident in Britain, 1951, 1961, 1971, 1981

	1951	1961	1971	1981
Total	10,208	41,898	73,295	84,327
Females	3,714	18,430	33,870	39,742
Males	6,494	23,468	39,425	44,585

Source: GRO (1956, 1964); OPCS (1974, 1983)

London representative of the then Turkish Federated State of Cyprus estimated that there were 50,000-80,000 Turkish Cypriots in Britain. More recent sources estimate the mainland Turkish and Cypriot speaking population to be around 150,000 (Mehmet Ali, 1991; Reid *et al*, 1999).

Because of the lack of separate data on Turkish Cypriot migration and the similarities between Turkish and Greek Cypriot outward movements from Cyprus, the Turkish Cypriot migration is analysed within general Cypriot migration patterns, which can be explained in three main stages (Alkan and Costantinides, 1982).

1 A small pre World War One migration

The first immigrants from Cyprus were mostly young men of Greek origin arriving as British subjects when Cyprus was a Crown Colony with a subsistence agricultural economy (Taylor, 1988). These were thought to be single men, students, seamen or merchants, who came to Britain for a better life (Constantinides, 1977). After the depression the British government promoted an alluring image of prosperity in England. In reality an applicant needed to have £30 for deposit, an ability to speak some English, certainty of work and friends and relatives who could guarantee accommodation and support. With the arrival of an increasing number in 1930s, an estimated 8,000 Cypriots were in full employment in the UK at the outbreak of the Second World War (Taylor, 1988).

Post war migration (1945-1974):

Major migration started after the Second World War, due to the hostilities on the island during the 1950s and early 1960s. This was when Turkish Cypriot migration started and the numbers mirrored the ratio of Turkish and Greek speakers in Cyprus (George and Millerson, 1967). Oakley's (1970 and 1971) demographic data is the main source of analysis of immigration into Britain.

Migration from Cyprus increased after Cyprus became a British colony in 1878. People who arrived during this period and later during the early 1950s were mainly from rural parts of Cyprus. This was a reaction to the rapid urbanisation process on the island which had started since the early 1950s. Constantinides (1977) found that most of the migrants from the two Greek Cypriot villages were from landless families with small non-viable holdings, typically young men with only elementary school education, no formal training and often already married with a young family.

The year 1960-61 saw the peak of migration, with 25,000 Cypriots entering Britain (Oakley, 1970). Ladbury (1977) has described how for the Turkish Cypriots, migration was a matter of personal choice for the individual, who regarded it as an economic opportunity rather than a necessity to support relatives by re-mittance. She claimed that the Turkish Cypriot migration repre-sented a cross section of the population. Generally the migrants were young – about half were under 35 – some single men and women, although many were already married but came alone and sent for their wives a year or two later. Migration was slowed by the 1962 Immigration Act.

2 Post-1974 migration

By the 1970s, people were coming to Britain from Cyprus, this time as refugees because of the war on the island. In July 1974 a short-lived coup, supported by the then ruling military junta of Greece, tried to overwhelm the Makarios government and its policy for an independent Cyprus. Fighting broke out between rival Greek factions and then between Greeks and Turks. To protect the 120,000 strong Turkish minority, Turkish forces from the mainland intervened justifying their action in accordance with the tripartite agreement made when the Republic of Cyprus was established in 1960. But to the Greeks this was an unjustified act of aggression. The inter-communal fighting and the subsequent population exchanges culminated in the division of the island into the Turkish North and the Greek South. It was significant reason for large numbers of Cypriots to leave for the UK. Most refugees were Greek Cypriots who had lost their homes and hoped to build a new life in the UK. An estimated 10,000-12,000 refugees arrived as the result of the war (Swann Report, 1985; World University Service, 1977, Clough and Quarmby, 1978).

By the 1990s the Turkish Cypriot migration from Cyprus was increasingly motivated by economic hardship, and emigration from the island was increasing not just to Britain but also to other countries in Europe, North America and Australia. It is estimated that the Turkish Cypriot population in England now equals the remaining Turkish Cypriot population in Cyprus – around 60,000 (Mehmet Ali, 2001).

Table 2 shows the number of entries from Cyprus between years 1975-1991, after which no census data are available. It included many people who had returned to Cyprus to retire and had lost everything during the war and had to start afresh. Some of these, who were never officially recognised as 'refugees', only stayed a short while and returned home, sometimes under threats of deportation due to *ad hoc* government policies (Gordon, 1983). But some 2,000-3,000 visitors and British passport holders remained to start a new life (Anthias, 1983).

The figures under 'British Citizenships' represent the number of Cypriot people who have retained their British nationality either through the 1960 Constitution or later by working in British bases as official employees of the British Government. These people performed various duties such as Auxiliary Police or semi-skilled/skilled jobs such as barbers, bakers, painters and plumbers inside the bases. The figures may also include their children who later obtained British nationality through their parents. The data gives us no information about the proportion of Turkish and Greek Cypriots in the total numbers. There are no accurate records of migration from 1991 to the present but unofficial records support the view that Turkish Cypriot migration from Cyprus has increased due to economic hardship, not just to Britain but to other countries in Europe (France, Germany, Belgium) and North America as well as Australia.

Settlement patterns in the UK
There are small Turkish communities scattered around the UK, for example in Manchester, Edinburgh and the Midlands, but the majority live in or around London. The initial Cypriot com-

Table 2: Migration in 1975-1991 of people born in Cyprus		
Years	All Citizenships	British Citizenships
1975	1096	655
1976	1498	775
1977	738	365
1978	707	483
1979	497	-
1980	607	-
1981	204	-
1982	198	184
1983	1123	-
1984	82	82
1985	1261	75
1986	3101	2591
1987	1705	1527
1988	2357	90
1989	2447	-
1990	-	-
1991	2052	1544
Total	19674	8371
Grand Total	28045	

Source: International Passenger Survey: OPCS (1995)

munities were established around Camden, Finsbury Park, Angel, Islington, Stoke Newington, Deptford and Camberwell in London. Turkish Cypriots have now moved on to Haringey, Enfield and other outer London boroughs.

The Turkish Cypriot community is part of the London way of life. As well as the kebab shops and the supermarkets, bakers, boutiques, video shops, insurance agencies, dry cleaners, cafes and restaurants, there are successful large businesses in import and export and the clothing industry. The Green Lanes district in North London is the main centre of economic and cultural activity for the community and is known as the *Capitol*. Whereas most first generation Turkish speaking settlers are employed in the traditional migrant economic activities they took over from Asians and Jews, the second and third generations are increasingly moving outside these traditional niches. There are increasing numbers of students from Cyprus and Turkey, though because of the economic difficulties in Cyprus, the numbers of Turkish Cypriot students at British universities has fallen considerably over the past decade.

Mainland Turks

Turkish mainland migration to Britain was an extension of the wider migration to Europe and began in the early1950s. The expanding European economy during the boom years of the 1950s and 1960s needed a workforce from other countries. It was Germany – West Germany up until 1990 – who received the first *legal workers* from Turkey (Issa, 1987).

There is little information about migration patterns to England. The mostly legal worker population arrived during the 1970s, followed by their families during the late 1970s and 1980s. It is estimated that 4,000 or so mainland Turks – only a fraction of Turkish workers in Europe – were working mainly in the catering and clothing industries (Paine 1974; Berger, 1975). Work permits had to be renewed every year. These workers are the parents and grandparents of the second and third generation Turkish speaking children in our schools today. They became residents after five years legal residence in Britain. Many still retain their Turkish nationality, mainly to protect their rights in Turkey, as according to Turkish Law, nationals who give up their citizenship lose certain rights, such as the right to own land there. Recent developments in the Turkish National Assembly have changed this legislation.[1]

Mainland Turks settled in areas like Haringey, Newington Green, Hackney, Stoke Newington and Wood Green, where there were already small businesses run by Turkish Cypriots. More recently mainland Turks have also acquired small businesses and bought their own homes in outer districts such as Enfield and Essex.

Turkish speaking Kurds

Kurds in the UK are from Iraq, Iran and Turkey. The different dialects of Kurdish they speak are not always mutually understandable. Although I refer to social, political and cultural relationships between the groups, the primary focus in this book is on the Kurds from Turkey.

Kurdish migration to Britain was political as well as economic. The first Kurdish refugees came in small numbers in 1958 (Dick, 2002). They were from Iraq (Wahlbeck, 1997) as well as Turkey. The main bulk of Kurdish migration began with a first wave in the 1980s because of the military coup in Turkey, and by late in the decade it had increased because of persecution by Sunni fundamentalists in Alevi dominated areas (McDowall, 1989; Collinson, 1990; Reilly, 1991).

The Kurds immigrated to the UK in three phases. The first was between 1987 and Spring 1988, during which time they overtook the Tamils as the principal asylum applicants in the UK. The government's response was detention and imprisonment, on the assumption that Kurds were 'economic migrants' rather than *bona fide* refugees (Griffiths, 2002:85). The second period covers May 1989 until the imposition of visas on 23rd June 1989[2], when entry was seen as an attempt to beat the enforcement of visa restrictions that would follow (Collinson, 1990, p29). The third migration was marked by the imposition of the visa requirements as well as the ascendancy of PKK affiliated organisations during the early part of the 1990s, in the Turkish-Kurdish community in North London (Griffiths, 2002, p86).

Settlement patterns

Due to a colonial link between Iraq and Britain, the initial settlement of Iraqi Kurds during the 1950s and 60s, and later during the 1991 Gulf War, tended to be within the established Iraqi community in West London (Wahlbeck, 1997; Al-Rasheed, 1994). Later settlements after 1980 of Turkish speaking Kurds in areas such as Hackney and Haringey were encouraged by the Turkish Cypriot economy in the garment and catering trades (Hackney Council, 1993). Iranian asylum seekers from the Islamic revolution in 1979 made up the largest single asylum applications in the late 1970s and early 1980s. An estimated 30,000 to 50,000 Kurds have applied for asylum since the late 1980s. Earlier estimates of the number of Kurdish settlers living in London was given as around 15,000 (Warner, 1991). However, with the aftermath of the Gulf War and the brutal actions of Saddam Hussein's regime, these numbers rose to 50,000 (Badcock, 2002). Wahlberg (1997, p172) estimates this to be around 30,000. There are about 4000 to 5000 Iraqi Kurdish asylum seekers in Birmingham alone (Dick, 2002). One of the problems with identifying accurate figures for Kurdish speakers is that they are not categorised as a distinct nationality or ethnic group and generally appear under the single category 'Turkish'.[3]

Marcuse (1996) describes Kurds from Turkey as forming 'enclaves' – not 'ghettos', which would be negative (1996:38). He points out the factors encouraging enclave formation: the political situation in Turkey imposed insularity born of the need to preserve Kurdish culture and identity. Griffiths (2002:88) refers to the perception of Kurds as 'being continually underestimated as a culture and a distinct nation' within local settlement contexts that appear to be outweighed by the national independence at home.

I explore the culture and identity of Kurdish speakers in the next chapter, with particular reference to language.

Notes

1 A recent agreement between Germany the country with the largest Turkish speaking population and Turkey made it possible for some people to hold dual citizenship.

2 The introduction of visas was seen as a response by the British authorities to the request from Germany, an EU partner to stop arrivals of Kurdish refugees who were allegedly entering Germany en route to Britain.

3 Although a few education authorities such as Hackney, Haringey and Enfield began categorising children in their schools as Turkish, Turkish Cypriot and Kurdish, this does not appear to be consistent throughout all the boroughs.

2

Language and identity

This chapter examines the language of the three groups of settlers described in chapter 1, and its uses and role in shaping inter-community group identities. I begin with Cypriot Turkish and follow with Turkish used by mainland Turks and, finally, Kurdish as used by the Turkish speaking mainland Kurds.

Turkish language

Turkic languages are spoken by around 100 million people, most of them living in an arc stretching from the Balkans through Central Asia to the borders of China. These languages share a similar agglutinative structure (Stubbs, 1985:67) and are to some extent mutually intelligible. About 50 million speak a Turkish standard form based on the speech of the educated elite of Western Turkey. Until the break-up of the Ottoman Empire after World War One, Turkish was written in the Arabic script, and Persian and Arabic lexical content was also very high. However, as part of Atatürk's westernising reforms in the 1920s, there was a switch to a modified Roman alphabet for written Turkish, and in the last twenty years moves were made to replace non-Turkish loan words with Turkic equivalents, a 'purification' process which appears to have been stepped up again (CILT 1983).

This process was in part the linguistic reflection of the move to a more narrowly nationalistic position after the Ottoman period ended but also part of a process of linguistic 'democratisation' –

an attempt to create a written standard language more accessible to less educated people. By the late Ottoman period the gap was considerable between the language of the sophisticated Istanbul elite and that of the Anatolian peasant farmers. Atatürk's reforms went some way to closing that gap. (Stubbs, 1985).

Cypriot Turkish

The Turkish Cypriot variety of Turkish is a derivative form of the Ottoman Turkish used by the 20,000 soldiers sent there to settle with their families after the island was conquered by the Ottomans in 1571. However, the most obvious influence is from Greek as the two communities lived side by side for centuries. A classic example is the well-known mani ballad which is made up of both languages:

ehtes, broktes, andibroktes	(yesterday, the day before and the day before that
ben duvardan bakardım	I was looking through the wall
ehela narto mesa	I wanted to come in but
ama anandan korkardım	I was afraid of your mum).

Cypriot Turkish has many words of Greek origin:

agsona	(Axle of a vehicle)
ahristo	(something which no longer has any use)
aligundi	(state of being paranoid)
argaci	(narrow waterway, small arch)
alizavra	(lizard)

This is also the case for Cypriot Greek, where many words are borrowed from Turkish.

As the result of British rule (from 1878 until 1960) Cypriot vocabulary has also been influenced by English, for example:

Isviç (switch)
referi (referee)
of (off)
fayıl (file)
celi (jelly)
roundabout

There are also Arabic, French and Italian influences on the Cypriot vocabulary.

Arabic:	*abes* (words uttered for no reason)
	acuze (old and tattered woman)
	fellah (gypsy)

French:	*managul* (nail varnish)
	basbartu (sticky paper)
	hartuş (paper bag)
Italian:	*gambana* (bell)
	gargola (bed)
	garudsa (horse driven carriage)

Source: E. Saracoğlu (1992)

Cypriot Turkish differs from the standard Turkish language of the educated elite in several ways. Some words used in Turkey have gone through transformation and have different meanings in Cypriot vocabulary, as illustrated below. Fundamental differences also exist in sentence construction between the two varieties. Under the influence of English, Cypriot Turkish has inverted construction patterns. In addition, the verb form changes. For example, note the changes in the word *gitmek* (to go) in the following example:

Cypriot Turkish

Lazım gideyim yarın Lefkosa'ya
I need to go tomorrow Nicosia.

Standard Turkish

Yarın Lefkoşa 'ya gitmem lazım
Tomorrow Nicosia I need to go

Other differences also occur in the structure of questions. Standard Turkish always uses the suffix – mi? or mu? to change the sentence into a question:

Çocuk okula gidiyor. The child goes to school.
Çocuk okula gidiyor mu? Does the child go to school?.

There are also differences in vowel sounds. Those in Cypriot Turkish resemble the varieties found in Anatolia today, following the conquest of the island in 1571 when the first settlers were brought from these regions. The main sound differences discussed here are with the Istanbul variety, which is taken as the standard written Turkish form.

The vowels used in Cypriot Turkish are generally the same as those used in Standard Turkish as the long vowels are used with words imported from other languages, but, these are pronounced shorter in Cypriot Turkish, as illustrated here:

Table 3

Standard Turkish	Cypriot Turkish
târih	tarih
kâtip	katip

There are differences between the use of the so called 'straight vowels' as in *a* and *e*.

a: thick wide and straight.
e: thin, wide and straight.

a	>	e	*meaning*
ahali		ehali	crowd
vasiyet		vesiyet	will (as in writing ones will)
masal		mesel	story
bahane		behane	excuse

a: think, wide and straight.
ı: thick, narrow and straight.

a	>	ı	
çağir		çığır	call (calling someone)
acaba		acıba	I wonder if..
fırça		fırçı	brush

Differences found in the so-called 'round wovels' as in *u* and *o*.

u: thick, narrow and round
o: thick, wide and round

u	>	o	
ufak		ofag	small
uğraş		oğraş	try
unut		onut	forget (it)

ü: thin, narrow and round
ö: thin, wide and round

ü	>	ö	
üfür		öfür	blow (blowing the candle)
yürü		yörü	walk
kümes		kömes	hen house

Source: E. Saraçoğlu (1992)

The two varieties also differ in the use of expressions which are sometimes puzzling to an Istanbul Turk. This is the result of some words losing their traditional meaning and being adopted to mean something completely different, for example:

Table 4

Word	Standard Turkish Meaning	Cypriot Turkish Meaning
kurtarmak	To save (as in saving someone's life)	To serve (as in serving food)
tutmak	To hold (as in holding a pen)	To be married (to somebody)

Cypriot Turkish shows similar patterns to the Greek Cypriot variety in having no suffix at the end of the sentence but simply prolonging the last tone in the last vowel (last word) of the sentence.

'*Does the child go to school?*' has similar construction patterns in Greek and Turkish:

Greek Cypriot
Do moron scoleon digenni.
Do moron scoleon digenni? (The accent on final syllable *-nni* turns it into a question).

Turkish Cypriot
Çocuk okula gider.
Çocuk okula gider? (The accent on final syllable *-er* turns it into a question).

Turkish Cypriot identity

One of the clear impressions emerging from the research literature on first generation Turkish Cypriot adults is the significance of Turkish in maintaining their identity (Taylor, 1988). In the ALUS (Adult Language Use Survey), Turkish Cypriots were almost unanimous in agreeing on maintaining the fullest use of Turkish in Britain (Linguistic Minorities Project, 1985). This is still the case today. Most of the Turkish Cypriot parents I have to spoken during my supplementary school visits appear to confirm this. Learning Turkish is still seen as a tool for transmission of cultural values and maintaining Turkish identity. Parents also point out that one of the reasons for their frequent visits to Cyprus is to enable their children to maintain the cultural links as well as provide opportunities for their children to practice their Turkish. One of the Management Committee members of the recently formed *Consortium for Turkish Supplementary Schools* told me that the number of pupils attending their schools has increased in recent years.

Earlier studies suggest that children prefer to speak Turkish amongst their peers in mainstream schools (Ulug, 1981). However, more recent findings suggest that the younger generations mainly use English in peer group interactions. Turkish is used to interact with their parents, grandparents or with their teachers in supplementary schools (Issa, 1993). The speech patterns also suggest a mixing of Turkish and English, creating a distinctive *Londralı* (Londoner) Turkish (Adalar, 1997). It is argued that mixed codes are indicative of a changing purpose where language is increasingly used to reflect a particular social/cultural experience (Issa, 2004b).

Turkish supplementary schools

Educational provision for the Turkish communities, as for many other groups establishing themselves in a host society, is mainly provided by the community supplementary schools. The main aim of these schools was to promote mother tongue teaching and preservation of Turkish culture (Memdouh, 1981). The Cyprus Turkish Association, established in 1951, began organising Turkish mother tongue classes from since 1959 in rented school premises in North London and there was further demand by the Turkish Cypriot communities in south London. The Cyprus Turkish Association has received limited support – mainly teachers from Cyprus or Turkey seconded for two or three years – from related Governments and has relied on financial support from the Turkish Cypriot community. From 1976 onwards the Turkish Federated State of Cyprus as well as the Turkish Government provided support in terms of teachers and teaching materials. However, there were issues around the suitability of materials and the particular teaching approaches used by some teachers employed by the Turkish and Turkish Cypriot embassies. This is an ongoing debate.

Today, supplementary schools are either funded by community organisations or jointly with the local LEAs. During the '70s and

'80s some mainstream primary and secondary schools provided mother tongue classes in addition to community supplementary schools, but only very few. The Schools' Council's survey of 1983 found that out of 23 LEAs providing mother tongue classes, Turkish was supported in seven schools. These classes were gradually phased out after the introduction of the Ethnic Minority Achievement Grant (EMAG). Currently in London, about thirteen schools function fairly independently. With few exceptions, these schools are set up to serve the specific aspirations of the communities: teaching aspects of Turkish culture and standard Turkish is seen as the key to all aspects of learning. There are major efforts from some sections of the community to try and preserve traditional Turkish cultural values.

Teaching children the 'correct' form of Turkish – mainly standard Turkish – is seen as crucial. While the importance of learning Standard Turkish is recognised, it is criticised by some educators who argue that the path to achieving this should be through recognition of the language varieties spoken by the children. There is also criticism of the materials used as not reflecting the children's experiences of everyday life in England. For children of Cypriot and Kurdish origin, this appears to present particular problems, particularly of identity, and fails to address the fundamental issue of academic achievement. This difficulty is particularly significant in relation to the use of the Turkish Cypriot variety (Issa, 2004b). When reminded to speak the 'correct' form of Turkish, children begin to doubt their own Turkish variety and this can undermine their self-image and seriously affect their learning. The issues for the Kurdish children are discussed the final part of this chapter. This is an area of ongoing debate between Turkish speaking educators. The other area of contention relates to the use of mixed code of Turkish and English in Cypriot speech patterns, which some see as language shift leading to erosion and to the final disappearance of a language (Fishman, 1991).

One school of thought regards Cypriot Turkish as the 'incorrect' form of the Standard Turkish or 'pigeon' Turkish. Others see it as the development of a new form of 'mixed' Cypriot Turkish adapting to a 21st century urban context (Dirim and Hieronymus, 2003; Issa, 2004b forthcoming). Lack of appropriate teaching materials coupled with insufficient training for too many supplementary school teachers generate difficulties for Turkish Cypriot children[1] and this negatively affects children's social and emotional development as well as their academic performance. The content of teaching and materials used, mostly imported from Turkey or Cyprus, generally tends to favour standard Turkish. Consequently, teachers face the challenge of trying to teach British born children of Cypriot Turkish parents to speak, read and write in standard Turkish.

An alternative approach is to use Cypriot Turkish as the main focus for developing the use of Standard Turkish. The outcome of such practices results in a 'Turkish' component being much more visible than the 'Cypriot' aspect of Turkish Cypriot identity in schools.[2]

My own observations in mainstream and supplementary schools appear to confirm this. I noticed that most pupils wore jewelry with the star and crescent and displayed Turkish flags on their books and bags. Most of the children told me they were proud to be Turkish. The whole ethos of the schools appeared to foster such pride. The majority of the parents I spoke to cite 'learning their language and culture' as one of the reasons for bringing their children to supplementary schools. Mainland Turkish speaking children attend the same supplementary schools as Cypriot Turkish speaking pupils and share similar experiences of supplementary schooling in the UK. However, as the speech varieties used by the children reflect regional variations from Turkey this raises similar issues relating to learning Standard Turkish. Again starting from children's own speech variations would be advantageous to their learning. However, it should be noted that such variations in speech patterns do not raise similar issues of identity for Mainland Turkish speakers, despite regional differences. Unlike in Kurdish and Turkish Cypriot varieties there are no significant differences in grammatical structures between standard Turkish and the regional spoken varieties found in Turkey. The difference is more in the vocabulary, pronunciation and semantics.

Turkish speaking mainland Kurds

Kurdish is an Indo-European language, most closely related to Persian and Luri. There are two main Kurdish dialects: Kurmanji and Sorani. Kurmanji is spoken in Turkey and in Iraq northwards from Mosul to the Caucasus and is written in Roman and Cyrillic scripts (Rutter, 2003). Until very recently, the Kurdish language was banned in Turkey. For this reason it has remained essentially a spoken language amongst the 14 million Kurds living in Turkey.

Kurds in the UK are from Iraq, Iran and Turkey. The numbers of Kurds from mainland Turkey is estimated to be 38,000 (Rutter, 2003) making it the largest of the three groups. Seventy five per cent of Kurdish refugees from Turkey are from rural parts of Turkey and mainly speak Kurdish at home. During my recent visit to a London Kurdish centre *Londra Halkevi* I spoke to the co-ordinator Yashar Ismailoğlu, who is also a specialist in Kurdish affairs. I asked him about the level of Kurdish literacy in the community. He told me that Kurdish was essentially a spoken language, Kurdish and Turkish being spoken at home. The younger generations speak Kurdish at home because this is the only language they can communicate in with their parents. Most Kurdish children are already literate in Turkish as they attended school in Turkey. Some attend Turkish or Kurdish supplementary schools in London. There are also community run Kurdish classes such as those run by *Londra Halkevi.*

Arrivals from the main urban centres in Turkey are less likely to speak Kurdish as their main language as these are second and third generation Kurds whose parents and grandparents migrated to big cities many years ago.

Although many scholars have noted the mutual unintelligibility between different dialects of Kurdish (Bruinessen, 1996; Kreyenbroek, 1992), Ismailoğlu disagrees, citing examples of Kurmanji and Dimilki (Zaza) speakers from Turkey communicating with Sorani speakers from Iraq by means of Kurmanji. This is supported by Griffiths' account of his interview with Turkish Kurds (2002:140).

Kurdish identity

Although all Kurds can claim areas of common experiences e.g. language, shared territory and religion, most Kurds perceive the 'common experience of suffering' as the basis for a shared sense of Kurdish identity (Griffiths, 2002, p131). In fact it is useful to mention that many Kurdish people I have spoken about this project have reminded me gently and firmly that the Kurds in Britain and indeed elsewhere do not accept being categorised as 'Turkish speaking communities'. Ismailoğlu made this point also during my visit to *Halkevi.* This position can be described in terms of

Turner's notion of 'community of suffering' (1957, p302) in which the affliction of each is of the concern for all. According to Ismailoğlu, the use of Turkish by most Kurds is an unavoidable consequence of having been denied of their Kurdish language. For the younger generation being in the UK is described as discovering one's own Kurdish identity. Griffiths' conversation with a young Kurdish woman who grew up in London can be broadened to adapt to other Kurds with similar experiences in London:

> You want to adopt it as well, become part of London, so to speak. I think the Kurds have the same problem. On top of that they've also got the struggle of trying to define themselves as Kurdish. Trying to define themselves as being Kurdish, *becoming Kurdish* (her emphasis) (Griffiths, 2002 p 137)

For most young Kurds in London this discovery of identity involves learning Kurdish while continuing to communicate in Turkish and English. Despite the attempts to 'reclaim' their Kurdish identity, many younger generation Kurds assert their superior competence in Turkish. As we saw, this is due to their education and subsequent integration into mainstream Turkish culture in Turkey. Because of this and economical factors involving all three communities, Turkish has emerged as the language of economic activity in the dynamic intra-cultural ethnic economy, as we shall see in the next chapter.

Kurdish language teaching

The use of Kurdish is widespread and most Kurdish children, especially those from rural areas of Eastern Turkey, start school with Kurdish as their first language. In England, a major dilemma facing Kurdish children in the mainly Turkish dominated supplementary schools is the lack of provision for teaching Kurdish. This state of affairs puts Kurdish children at a further disadvantage as they try to cope with learning two languages (Turkish and English) without maintaining and developing their Kurdish.

There are some organised network of classes for children and adults to promote Kurdish language and culture. Four of these were organised by *Halkevi*, and included a training course for Kurdish teachers and a theatre group, organised for the specific purpose of presenting plays 'to utilise Kurdish culture and language' (*Halkevi-Malagel* Bulletin 2003). Classes In Kurdish are usually held after school or at weekends for children and in the evenings for adults. In addition, some Kurdish children attend Turkish supplementary schools. There they are often categorised as being 'from Turkey', along with other children from the mainland. Although their Kurdish identity is recognised, teaching takes place in the medium of Turkish. Rutter (2003) identifies seven community schools that teach Kurdish as well as Turkish. Other community-based classes are run by organisations such as KWA, as well as by the communities themselves. But provision is often patchy and appears to lack a coherent strategy. Fesih Eren, an Education Adviser for the Kurdish community also highlighted this point in conversation (10 May 2004). Dr Eren pointed out that community organisations should implement a more coherent and unified strategy to support Kurdish language maintenance in the UK.

Kurdish children as refugees in British schools

The Refugee Council estimated that about 15,000 asylum seeking and refugee children failed to secure a school place in the UK. According to the report 60 per cent of these were fourteen to sixteen year old new arrivals (Refugee Council, 2000). Like many other refugee communities, Kurdish children attending British schools suffer from inadequate English language support, racism and bullying. Researchers for a study in Hackney (1995) interviewed thirty-two refugee children from a range of communities including Bosnians, Turkish Kurds, Somalis and Vietnamese. All the children were judged by their teachers to be 'coping' in school but nineteen of them reported that they had suffered racial harassment and nine had moved school (Rutter, 2003). Apart from a few LEAs, Kurdish speaking children are placed in the category 'Turkish' in Standard Attainment Tests (SATs).

The use of Turkish by most of the Kurdish speakers – despite its use at home – needs to be linked to historical events and the dominance of Turkish for generations in Turkey. Dr. Eren observed how this persists in the UK, where many Kurds who are competent in Kurdish choose to speak Turkish amongst themselves, especially in Turkish dominated parts of London. This preference, along with other intra-ethnic social variables, supports the dominance of Turkish as the language of economic interaction amongst the three communities, Turkish, Kurdish and Cypriot.

The use of Turkish and its varieties in the UK

The Linguistic Minorities Project, an extensive research study on language use amongst the communities in London during the 1980s (Reid *et al*, 1985) reported that first generation Cypriot parents believed strongly in maintaining and supporting Turkish as the mother tongue of their children. However, only two-fifths of them thought there were no problems with maintaining their language. The parents thought that the authorities should make provision within the mainstream to support teaching of Turkish (Taylor, 1988). With the abolition of the Inner London Education Authority (ILEA) in 1990, provision for mother tongue maintenance within mainstream schools decreased dramatically. Today, the use of Turkish within Turkish speaking households is still relatively strong, as a great majority of the Turkish speaking children start school having heard and spoken mainly Turkish at home. The increase in the use of English in Cypriot households is directly affecting the use of Turkish: children from Cypriot backgrounds understand English as well as Turkish when they start school. There is increasing evidence of borrowings and switching between the two languages. This apparent change in Cypriot Turkish is so noticeable that the term *Londralı Turkish* has been coined to describe it (Adalar, 1997).

These borrowings are the product of specific working environments which are then reinforced at home. They can easily be detected in the language of economic interaction, for example:

İsterim iki tane overlock'*cu.*   (I need two over-lookers)
Koyun tek tek bundle'*ları.*   (Put the bundles separately in ones)
Ben finisher'*ciyim.*   (I am a finisher)

Some evidence also suggests other similarities with nouns from English (Adalar, 1997):

Yarın shopping'*e gideceğim* (I will go shopping tomorrow)
Bugün off'*um* (I am off today). (M.Ali, 1991)

These are typical Cypriot speech patterns that have accommodated natural change brought about by being in a host country. It is not yet clear how much mainland (spoken) Turkish and Kurdish has adapted the *Londralı* Turkish patterns.

Londralı Turkish in the workplace therefore enables the linguistically distinct communities to function within a mutually accepted standardised form. This should be recognised not simply as serving a communicative purpose, as the languages are not really dissimilar, but more importantly as a language of social and community integration and interaction. In some ways it represents the specific and sometimes unique experiences of Londralı Turkish in the workplace and serves to unify people who have varying experiences and forms of spoken Turkish. Above all it represents – especially to the generation born in the UK – the experiences of being a multilingual Briton communicating through the medium of Turkish, and it serves as the language of social/economic interaction between the various communities. Children's linguistic and conceptual development is enhanced as the result of these interactions. Through their involvement in family businesses and economically oriented talk at home, children can more readily develop particular concepts (Issa, 2002). Sadly however, the social and economic experiences which occur in Turkish are largely ignored in both mainstream and supplementary schools. I argue that this should be reconsidered, and go on to explore children's understanding of economic concepts through bilingual interaction.

Notes

1 One of the areas of difficulty for Cypriot children is the insistence of some teachers from Cyprus on the use of 'correct form' of Turkish despite their own Cypriot roots.

2 It is useful to point out that activities such as arts and cultural events (e.g. folklore dancing, drama) are more frequently used to represent what may be called traditionally 'Cypriot' customs and characteristics.

3

Economic understanding and cultural context in learning

Children's linguistic and conceptual development is, as I have indicated, enhanced by their interactions and involvement in family businesses. At intra-community level at least, this interaction takes place in Turkish. In this chapter I explore children's understanding of economic concepts through bilingual interaction. First, I look at family life and community activities.

Family life and Structure

The family is of great importance to Turkish speaking communities. Earlier research (Oakley, 1968,1979; LCSS, 1967) described the traditional village society family lifestyles and values in which Cypriots had their roots. Post-war life in Cyprus, with its new economic and educational opportunities, especially in the towns, was already changing as the migrants left in the 1950s and 1960s (Taylor, 1988). Family ties were extended and loosened by emigration itself. In Cyprus urban and rural life were in sharp contrast, in terms of employment, education, social interaction and the pace of life (George, 1960; LCSS, 1967; Butterworth and Kinnibrugh, 1970). The majority of migrants came from the villages – communities of 200-2,000 – where life was centred upon coffee houses, school and special events (such as weddings, football matches). The village communities 'demanded of their members fairly rigid adherence to a set of social practices and associated values' (Constantinides, 1977, p23) which were closely associated with family honour, loyalty and kinship ties and 'gender-differentiated cultural ideals' (Oakley, 1979, p17), especially the 'sexual purity' of women (Anthias, 1983).

A Cypriot village is made up of small autonomous family groups, closely connected by ties of marriage and descent. The family is a nuclear unit of married parents and their children, plus possibly elderly or widowed grandparents. A married brother and his family may live in the same household, but each family aims to be a sovereign and self-reliant unit (Taylor, 1988). Family loyalty 'a paramount virtue' (Oakley, 1979) involves the obligation to put the immediate family and next of kin before others. Every individual member is expected to maintain and promote the honour, reputation and welfare of their family group by discharging roles and responsibilities in line with gender expectations. The male head of the family has a particular responsibility to represent the family in public and family life in the village. Conduct is very much open to public scrutiny and many individual problems are revealed and treated only within the family (Oakley, 1968).

The nuclear family and household is usually established on marriage. In Turkish and Kurdish families marriages were traditionally arranged between families in the same village by parents, sometimes with the help of a go-between, but now young people have more independence and initiative before their parents institute formal proceedings. Oakley (1968) observes that in traditional marriage practices, the economic social standing of the parents were evenly matched. Although these practices are still adhered to they are less rigid in practice and contrived to a small affluent group. This group consists of rich businessmen and women, professionals such as lawyers, doctors or politicians who often regard themselves as 'the elite' wishing to maintain their social status by facilitating the marriage of their sons and daughters. Amongst Turkish Cypriots in London in the 1970s marriages were no longer arranged between members of families who originally migrated from the same village in Cyprus, but certain kin relationships were strengthened and relationships were formed on the basis of status in the UK (Ladbury, 1977). As a marriage partner, a Turkish Cypriot would choose a fellow Cypriot brought up in Britain, on the assumption that they would have better understanding of one another. However the present marriage practices suggest that this has not necessarily continued but there is no evidence to suggest that divorce rates are higher amongst couples from Cyprus and Britain as opposed to couples who both come from Cyprus or Britain.

Within the patriarchal family structure of traditional Turkish and Kurdish households, there is a strict division of labour between husband and wife. She is under the authority of her husband, the source of family discipline. Within this traditional family structure certain expectations are held of sons and daughters.

Masculinity is emphasised in Turkish and Kurdish societies, as boys are seen as continuity of patronymy and as economic assets whereas girls require a dowry to take to their husbands' families. The mother is totally responsible for the children. Although she expects obedience, she is also the provider of emotional warmth and security and is close to her sons (Oakley, 1968). The father's fondness is shown more in symbolic interaction with the children, which takes precedence over the husband/wife relationship (Triseliotis, 1976). Babies and toddlers receive more indulgent attention but discipline is firmer by the age of four, so that they develop a sense of personal responsibility, morality and authority instilled by limited physical punishments, such as smacking. Older children are often responsible for their younger brothers and sisters. Childcare may also be shared with grandmothers, other relatives and neighbours. By time they go school, children are made to feel a wider responsibility to the family and they have adopted gender-differentiated duties on the land or at home as mini adults. These rules and responsibilities increase in adolescence, when young men are traditionally allowed greater freedom whereas the girls live a more home based life preparing for marriage – the final step to adult status (Taylor, 1988). Traditionally children remain economically and psychologically dependent on their parents until then. Only with the extension of the secondary education to the majority and the struggle for independence in Cyprus and consequent political upheavals leading to the introduction of military service for both Turkish and Greek Cypriots, has a concept of youth and adolescence developed (Oakley, 1968).

Since the post war migration from Cyprus and Turkey during the 1970s, there have been changes in the traditional patterns of family and social life. For example as more job opportunities became available to women with the expansion of certain sectors of the economy such as professional, service and manufacturing, the traditional roles ascribed to women in the towns have been changing. Women began contributing financially to the upkeep of their household. This has led to a reassessment by women of the traditional values and certainly led to a degree of financial independence. Change was much slower in the villages and has been maintained in some respects by Turkish speaking communities in the UK. This can be attributed to the first generation of migrants who saw themselves as being in an 'alien' country and the need to hold on to their cultural identity. This is changing with the second and the third generation in the UK. How these practices have been modified and changed was shaped by what individual families do. Again change is less evident in the villages, although the numbers of educated women has been increasing steadily. Generally there is still a sense of family solidarity although in the UK we are beginning to see cases of elderly, mainly Cypriot, men or women in old people's homes. In Cyprus traditional support systems are still maintained as extended families still live in close proximity.

Things are somewhat different in the case of Kurdish women. Due the to political situation over the Kurdish independence movement in Turkey and Iraq, many traditional child rearing practices ascribed to women have been abandoned in favour of the struggle for independence. Kurdish historian Izady (1992) has noted the marked independence of women in Kurdish society compared to other orthodox Muslim nations. For many Kurdish women being part of a political struggle has offered the possibility of 'personal and political achievement and a worthwhile sense of sacrifice' Laiser (1996, p190). The process has helped 'establish for themselves new identities, skills and respectable social positions, as well as to struggle for causes they believed in' (Yuval-Davis, 1997, p110).

For many Kurds migration to the UK resulted in change in the social conditions. Many Kurdish men and women lived in mainly rural areas in Turkey, Syria and Iraq. While making such adjustments to large urban contexts, they are still trying to maintain their cultural practices which they perceive as maintaining the cultural and biological reproduction of the community to contribute to the national cause back at home. To some women who were fighting alongside men in the mountains, this change presents further challenges. The issue has been one of adjustment to a new life in London:

> ...but now when we came here (London) when we struggle to adapt to this society, life is a struggle that we have to establish ourselves... Now we are back to the responsibilities of women and mother, children, family, domestic, everything. We go back to all these problems. And on top of that try and learn the language, find a job an then adapt to English society, to integrate. (Griffiths, 2002, p147)

Employment patterns in Turkey, Cyprus and the UK

In the present climate of unemployment and gender discrimination in Northern Cyprus and Turkey there are more opportunities for educated men than women. The exception is in rural Turkey where there is little change in terms of job opportunities for Kurdish men and women both. In households where both parents are from professional backgrounds and are in employment, grandparents or next of kin provide child-care support while both parents are at work.

The employment background from which many Turkish speaking communities came was that of an agrarian economy, based on small-holdings and families working in the fields. In Cyprus, the economic depression of the 1950s was followed in the 1960s by diversification, with increasing mechanisation of agriculture, which engaged 40 per cent of the economically active population. Industry, mining and tourism all developed (LCSS, 1967). The British military bases were also sources of employment. Nonetheless underemployment was widespread and families generally had small incomes. Urban developments encouraged some migration from rural areas into the towns. Generally women occupied themselves with household tasks, especially sewing, though in the 1960s some in the towns took up clerical work. Some men worked in towns before emigrating to Britain, but Oakley (1970) found that those with jobs stayed in Cyprus even if they had relatives abroad. Daniel (1968) found that seventy eight per cent of his sample in the UK had been working before they emigrated. The demographic report for Cyprus in 1963 (quoted by George and Millerson, 1967) showed that about a third of emigrants to the UK from 1959 to 1963 were craftsmen or tradesmen. About 15 per cent were in catering, but roughly half were classified as unskilled or had skills which might not be directly useful to them in the UK.

The post-war migrants came to join relatives and friends, most of whom were already established in catering. By 1945 there were 200 Cypriot restaurants in London, compared with 29 in 1939. By 1958 this figure rose to 350, alongside 182 hairdressers, 150 tailors, 78 grocers, 72 shoemakers and 38 other businesses. Oakley (1970) reported that, although Cypriots continued in the traditional skills and crafts, chiefly tailoring, hairdressing and shoemaking, retail trades especially grocery and greengrocery became increasingly popular. These, like catering, were newly acquired skills, often a response to the available opportunities but also motivated by the desire for independence rooted in traditional patterns. Yet as Anthias (1983) observed, many Cypriots were excluded from other openings because they lacked English language skills. Table 5 shows the percentage of Cypriot men in employment in 1966.

To this list for the 1960s, Alkan and Constantinides (1981) add greengrocers (retailing produce from Cyprus), grocers, butchers, patisseries, bakeries, dress factories, furniture shops. These wide ranging businesses constituted both an external and internal economy, predominantly the provision of personal services for the general public as well as for the communities.

Table 5: Socio-economic grouping of Cypriot men, compared with the whole of population in Greater London, 1966 (percentages)

	Whole population (%)	Cypriot men (%)
Professional workers	5.4	2.7
Employers and managers	11.8	11.0
Foremen, skilled manual and own-account workers (other than professionals)	34.1	41.8
Non manual workers	23.1	6.4
Personal service, semiskilled	14.3	31.2
Unskilled manual workers	8.1	7.0

Sources: Census, 1966; Collison, 1969

In the 1970s migrants from Turkey worked in restaurants and factories owned by Turkish Cypriots. Kurdish migration during the 1980s followed a similar pattern: these mainly unskilled workers were taken in by already established businesses run by Cypriots and later by mainland Turks. A slowing down of the clothing industry and their desire to have their own businesses saw many Kurds setting up supermarkets, groceries, butchers, kebab shops, restaurants and other small enterprises. In London, areas such as Newington Green, Haringey, Wood Green and Tottenham are full of Turkish/Kurdish shops open until late each evening.

Turkish speaking workers, especially new arrivals, understandably feel more secure working for someone with whom they can communicate in Turkish. So communal economic activity in Hackney, Newington Green, Haringey and Tottenham is particularly strong, especially in the clothing industry which is concentrated in these areas. Hackney and Haringey are the main areas of concentration for Kurds and Haringey, Wood Green and Tottenham for Turkish speaking Kurds (Haringey Council, 1997). These are the most deprived areas in the borough, with unemployment and other social issues among the highest in the country. New arrivals often rely on fellow countryfolk for job opportunities and other forms of support, thus the networking patterns incorporate them into the existing support system.

The community support system provides the newcomer with basic knowledge and skills on which they can quickly build. The relationship with the owner of a clothing factory, for example, is generally good as the employment works to mutual advantage – although there is an element of exploitation by the owner. The new worker may be aware of this but prefer a lower paid job among compatriots to a better paid job at first, at least until they feel confident enough to move on to something better.

The economic social structures created and supported by this process are economic enclaves, where the members are economically interactive and interdependent in a mutually created micro economy. Marcuse (1996) described enclaves as:

> Areas of spatial concentration which are walled in socially if not physically, but which have positive consequences for their residents. Marcuse 1996, p38

Although children of mainland Turkish and Cypriot parents are beginning to move outside the 'traditional' ethnic economy, this does not appear to be true of the young Kurdish speakers. Rutter's (1994) survey on refugees gave insight into young refugee children's aspirations for their own future job prospects. When asked what they wanted to do when they finished school, many Kurdish children said they wanted to do similar jobs to their parents, such as working in greengrocers, off licences and kebab shops. The survey supports the findings relating to lack of employment opportunities as perceived by young refugee children in the UK. It also strengthens claims that there is no social mobility amongst Kurdish refugees, especially the new arrivals.

Community activities

One of the ways in which Turkish speaking communities have sought to establish themselves in the UK is through various voluntary associations and social/cultural events intended to recreate and keep alive traditional cultural practices.

The Cyprus Turkish Association was established in 1951, partly to promote mother-tongue teaching and the preservation of Turkish Culture (Memdouh, 1981). Other organisations followed later such as the Turkish Islamic Association, the Ladies' Association and the Turkish Arts Society. During the late '70s several student political associations and organisations were set up to support various political parties in Northern Cyprus. Numerous village associations were formed by the people from villages in Cyprus to provide financial support for these villages. Similar associations supported towns and villages in Turkey and these village associations are also represented in the Turkish Football League. Towards the end of the 90s there were nearly 40 associations and clubs in London alone. Several attempts have been made to group these associations under a single body. The aim of the Council of Turkish Associations UK was to have a unified voice on issues concerning Cyprus and Turkey. The diversity of views and the power struggles within the Council prevented the group from functioning as a unified body but there is a successful Consortium of Turkish Supplementary Schools that co-ordinates thirteen schools. It aims to work on issues related to underachievement and design a common curriculum for all Turkish supplementary schools.

The dynamism of the communities is enhanced by the cultural activities between these groups. There is regular contact between the members of the communities in football matches in the Turkish community league. Turkish wedding parties, for example, are occasions where as many as five hundred guests may be invited and are a major cultural event for the community. Turkish newspapers and magazines provide culturally specific and relevant news for these communities. From 1959 a weekly Turkish newspaper has been available in England, printed in and supplied from Germany. Today five newspapers are printed in London and others from Turkey and Cyprus are distributed in the UK.

Although the newspapers fulfil the function of sharing community news, they do not appear to reach all sections of the community, particularly the young people who cannot easily read standard Turkish. Even Cypriot Turkish used in the *mizah*, the comic sections, is difficult to decode because it is not taught in supplementary schools and remains essentially a spoken language. The debate surrounding the use of Cypriot Turkish to support Cypriot speaking children's literacy development is a controversial one and continues to dominate discussions in supplementary schools.

At the centre of all community activities is *London Turkish Radio* (LTR), established over ten years ago and providing a variety of programmes for all sections of the communities. It is a platform for everyone to voice their opinions on aspects of political life here as well as in Cyprus and Turkey. Local businesses and shops can advertise their products and new initiatives. Cultural activities are announced and invitations issued to communities to attend functions. LTR contributes to the dynamism of the Turkish speaking communities and supports inter communal economic networks.

The Kurdish speaking community

When one talks about Turkish speaking Kurds in Britain, it is often difficult to separate their experiences from those of their fellow Kurds who arrived from Iran, Iraq, Lebanon and elsewhere. All are affected – and to a certain extent unified – by a common political cause. This is not to say that all Kurdish speaking people support the politics of the PKK, the Kurdish guerrilla organisation fighting for an independent Kurdistan. However, there is a sense of commonality of experience amongst Kurds in the UK (Grifffiths, 2002) in their quest to become an independent nation

(Bruinessen, 1992b). Organisations such as the *Halkevi*, Kurdish Community Centre (KCA) and Day-Mer centre in Hackney are nationalistic in character but they nonetheless fulfil many other social functions such as language teaching, drama activities, meetings and providing venues for wedding parties. *Halkevi* has a large hall in Hackney with a stage, library, a coffee shop and a giant screen showing Med TV, a Kurdish TV station, and the largest membership of Kurds in Europe, with nearly 15,000 members. Similarly Kurdish Workers Association (KWA) also organises many community based activities. These centres attract large Kurdish attendance regardless of political affiliation. MED TV, set up to preserve the Kurdish identity (Ryan, 1995), began broadcasting in May 1995 and uses a variety of languages including Arabic and minority dialects in addition to Kurdish and Turkish. As well as presenting music, cultural programmes and news, Med TV offers Kurds the chance to learn the classics in translation and buys in documentaries from the BBC, presented mainly in Kurmanji (Griffiths, 2002). There is also a Kurdish Radio station, *Rojbaj*, broadcasting two hours a day and broadcasting a variety of news, music and cultural programmes.

This brief account of the migration and employment patterns, social and cultural activities of the communities reveals some of the similarities and differences between them. With regard to Kurds for example, it reveals their perception of their own identity and language. One common area of experience is that Turkish is used as the language of inter-community interaction. This is now explored further with reference to economic activities within the communities and the consequent influence on children's development of economically related concepts.

The economic understanding of Turkish speaking children

Cypriot employment in the 'traditional industries' started from the early 1950s. By the 1960s, factories and shops were being be set up under Cypriot ownership. Migration ensured a constant supply of labour for these small businesses. The shared cultural values bonded the members of the community together in the host country. In order to survive the hostilities of a strange and alien country, members chose to live within close proximity. This close network of support generated community based economic activities which grew stronger with each new arrival, and became a thriving domestic economy.

The slowing down of Turkish Cypriot immigration in the late 1960s was replaced with arrival of mainland Turks in the 1970s. A significant number of these workers found employment in already established Turkish Cypriot businesses. After the 1980s, the arrival of Kurdish speaking people from mainland Turkey ensured a further supply of workers for the economy. These migration patterns not only contributed to the maintenance of a strong ethnic economy but also provided a dynamic and continuing economic culture.

As long as the products of this ethnic economy were in demand by the host community at large, the ethnic economic community functioned effectively. Also essential for maintaining strong community-based economic activities is a constant supply of labour. The experience of minorities in Britain shows that labour shortages have been quickly filled by migration, as illustrated by the Jewish experience in the clothing industry in the UK. As Jews fled Europe from the 1920s until the end of the Second World War, Jewish industries constantly received Jewish workers. When this migration slowed and ceased vacancies created as the workforce retired were gradually replaced by the new workforce from other communities. After the initial settling-in period, the new arrivals started to set up factories of their own and began employing people from their own communities. The present dynamic Turkish economy follows a similar pattern in its development.

Economic activities are the basis of the inner dynamism of the Turkish-speaking communities. Its members share similar cultural characteristics of language and customs. Turkish-speaking children encounter particular economic activities in closely linked community environments, and begin forming concepts related to those activities from even before they begin formal schooling. For Kurdish children who are exposed to these concepts at home, this process will operate in Kurdish at first. Children will be exposed to Turkish while working in their parents' shops or out shopping with them. So these economically related concepts will continue developing in Turkish. Before discussing this process further, it is useful to place the ideas behind it within a theoretical framework.

Being exposed to specific economic ideas does not necessarily lead to thorough understanding of that concept, nor does it develop in isolation from other concepts experienced in an environment. I argue that higher levels of participation by the children contribute to raising their levels of understanding. Differences encountered in children's understanding relate to their interpretation of activities, as children interpret each learning environment differently. Children are influenced by factors such as their individual development as well as their previous learning experiences. Children have different cognitive abilities and learning strategies.

These arguments are supported by studies on children's development as learners. Children's economic understanding does not take place simply as the child develops naturally; on the contrary, cultural factors play a significant part. Bruner (1972) pointed to the importance of the environment in the development of the child's intellect in general learning contexts. He viewed the development of cognition as 'adapting to the spurts of innovation ... transmitted by the agents of the culture' (1972 p165). Accordingly, the child processes information through interaction with the environment and through the use of specific language representatives of cultural experiences. Piaget viewed cognition as a universal phenomenon, while Bruner emphasised the role of language in learning. Bruner suggested that 'where there were language differences between learners, there might exist cognitive differences' (1972, p23) and he was among those who were convinced of the importance of language in affecting cognitive development (Vygotsky, 1962; Luria, 1973). These researchers argued that Piaget's experiments on cognitive development were limited to the experiences of Western European children (1972, p24). Bruner showed that certain characteristics common to most Western European cultures were absent in most non-Western ones and vice versa. For instance, Eskimo children who grew up under the influence of cultural values relating to subsistence culture developed natural cognitive mechanisms for collective group actions. Bruner drew our attention to the way these children developed their 'subordinate structures without the intervention of the kind of egocentricism we often observed in Western children' (1972, p 28).

The process of internalisation was held to depend on interaction with others, and 'upon the need to develop corresponding categories and transformations for communal action' (1972, p 166). Bruner pointed to the role of direct experience in the actual learning process. The more directly the child was involved with the environment, the more effective the learning process. Other factors in this process of internalising included the naming of each child's individual capability to interpret such experiences, such as the cognitive, psychological and linguistic ability of each child to relate to an experience.

Other research on children's economic understanding seemed to support Bruner's identification of cultural factors. Gustav Jahoda's (1983) work challenges Piaget's studies, suggesting that non-European children had a 'cultural lag', a slower or deficient rate of cognitive development (1983, p113). Jahoda investigated the notion of profit in the context of transactions and banking (1979). He interviewed 120 Scottish children between the ages of six and twelve. He constructed a shop transaction scene in a role-play situation in which he became a customer and a supplier and assessed the children's reasoning by asking questions to determine their understanding of the concept of profit. He found that children's reasoning ability became clearer as they grew older, but he noted that one reason for their lack of coherence was their unfamiliarity with the questions asked by the experimenters. Jahoda noted that the children, in trying to answer the questions, were constructing their understanding of events. He concluded that profit was a complex and difficult concept which children did not fully grasp until the age of eleven. Jahoda then repeated the same study on profit with a group of Zimbabwean children (1983). His aim was to show that the relative backwardness claimed about non-European children was due to their lack of familiarity with the issues, and that this would be reversed in situations where these children had appropriate experience. He found that thanks to their involvement in trade from an early age, Zimbabwean children showed a far superior understanding of the concept of profit than did their Scottish counterparts.

Other cross-cultural studies supported Jahoda's findings. Hong Kwang and Stacey's (1977) study with Malaysian-Chinese children from Hong Kong found that economic understanding developed in the same sequence in both Hong Kong and Western children. However, the level of understanding of children from Hong Kong was considerably more sophisticated and they showed an understanding of profit by age six and of how a bank worked by age ten. In a later study of 120 Malaysian-Chinese children, Tan and Stacey (1981) found a sequence of development in the acquisition of concepts similar to those of the Western children, even though the upbringing of Malaysian-Chinese children differed from that in the West. Their findings indicate that children follow a similar sequence in reasoning about economic concepts, but they seemed to grasp some concepts more quickly than others.

The role-play activities mentioned in the following chapters are considered in the theoretical framework just outlined. Children's active involvement in economic procedures enables such concepts to develop further within culturally specific contexts. Concepts can thus be seen as the products of particular economic environments. As will be shown, these economic experiences can have specific cultural focus, i.e. the type of economic concepts and the way children are exposed to them may vary significantly. However, the underlying principles of the development of such concepts show similar patterns across bilingual speech communities.

Accordingly, shop transactions of Turkish speaking children are analysed in relation to cross-cultural contexts. Turkish and Kurdish households foster the development of such culturally acquired concepts and provide a natural extension for the development of children's economic experiences within the communities. It is at home that children begin to form their initial understanding of economic concepts. In some Turkish and Kurdish households it is quite common to find that the daily routines of shopkeeping dominate conversation at the dinner table. It is not unusual for a child to witness a heated discussion over the cost of a garment delivered to the mother who works as a machinist at home.[1]

Independent businesses

Adamın kendi isi var. ('The man has his own work' – implying that the person has formed his own business).

'Having your own business' is a symbol of economic status within the community[2] and relates to the idea of 'making it' in Britain. A common topic of conversation between adults concerns their own businesses and how it could be improved. Children are often familiarised from an early age with the concepts relating to basic interactions in economic relations. Children also have links with the countries of origin of their parents and grandparents and, in regular visits, enhance their abilities in developing cross-cultural perspectives from an early age. These might include the difference in price between two identical items sold in the two countries, money and exchange mechanisms, profit etc. Some children spend a considerable time in their parents' shops, helping as well as witnessing transactions with the customers.

All these experiences contribute to children's understanding. Children develop economic concepts at different ages and their degree of participation in relevant activities can contribute significantly to their understanding of such concepts. This is explored in Part 2.

Notes

1 Although the numbers were quite high during the period of the study, the number of home-machinists has been steadily declining over the past years.

2 The origins of such beliefs goes back to Cyprus and Turkey where having your own business was a status symbol and was highly regarded within the communities.

PART 2

Language use in informal role-play settings

4
Children's understanding of cost

some of the ways children acquire economically related concepts have been discussed. When listening and sometimes taking part in children's conversations it was not difficult to identify the most widely used economic concepts. These were cost, money, buying and work.

Part 2 of the book looks at children's conversations and examines the development in their thinking relating to these economic concepts. But first I give some background information about the study.

The contexts for learning
My study concerns a particular group of bilingual children in London schools, all of whom are either second generation Cypriots or children of parents who came from Turkey to settle in Britain during the 1970s and 1980s.

Setting up the sample
The sample was chosen from a Hackney mainstream primary school where I had worked as a bilingual support teacher a few years ago. I selected children whose parents' occupations suggested exposure to discussions about economic activities. To analyse how children's concepts developed, I collected data at three monthly intervals. Role-playing activities were designed to encourage collaboration and to facilitate natural spoken language.

The school

The Hackney school was chosen for its solid reputation and multi-cultural ethos. It served diverse linguistic communities and was oversubscribed each year. The school had 230 children on roll and included a nursery as well as infant and junior classes. Children were given opportunities to extend their home languages in a variety of learning contexts created through in school and out of school activities. Bilingual children were encouraged to use their first languages. Assemblies and other activities were conducted in several languages and children were confident about using their own languages in the school.

I knew most of the staff as well as the children. The children in the study were from different classes and had not worked with me before. Their parents were involved in small businesses, such as in the clothing industry, restaurants, printing stores, kebab stores and groceries. Children told me they either helped their parents at work after school or waited in the work place until the workday ended. Some mothers worked at home as machinists. The children often talked about the daily routines of home and about what their mothers did and when they got paid.

Setting up the activities

Activities were identified that would allow the children's under-standing of economic concepts to be explored through progres-sively planned tasks. The activities were planned to generate dis-cussions that would help me look at children's interpretations and meanings regarding economic concepts. The use of Turkish and English was encouraged so the children would think in greater depth, as we knew they had experience of financial transactions in both languages in their family environments. The activities were sequenced to be increasingly demanding in terms of level of economic organisation. As activities became more demanding, discussions around these concepts was expected to intensify.

Usually, two stores were set up and the children encouraged to compete with each other. Recordings of the conversations were made simultaneously, using two tape recorders, at Store one (which they named Nicosia) and Store two (named Cappodocia). Each group had even numbers of girls and boys and the groups re-mained in the same stores throughout the study. This helped team efforts and collaboration, as the children discussed matters concerning buying and selling their products and pursuing the goal of making money for their stores.

Each session was planned to build upon learning in previous sessions and there was a natural progression in content. Topics were related to economic activities in Turkish households, workplaces and within the wider community. Children were familiar with the topics through their experiences at home and also from frequent visits to Turkey or Cyprus. Role-playing activities were devised to maximise collaboration and the sharing of economic experiences and to help establish group interactive processes that would use both languages. Because of their opportunities to explore concepts through collaborative activities, the children were expected to develop their understanding of these concepts far more rapidly than otherwise.

The collaborative activities facilitated interaction between the children: they were asked to negotiate and clarify roles and to act accordingly.[1] Through their interaction they negotiated roles in the stores, dispute settlement and collaborative teamwork. They also talked about issues that had little relevance to the activity but were significant in terms of the language used. They used generic, everyday language to express a point of view, while other language was specifically related to trade and economic concepts. The collaboration developed by setting a goal for the children by working together to achieve their goal, such as making more money than the rival store.

At the beginning of each activity, the children were reminded of what had happened in the previous session. I explained the main task for each session, facilitating interactions by posing relevant questions and helping the children to consider various possibilities. Occasionally I intervened to help them reflect on their thinking, by posing relevant questions. Thus, for example:

> Why has it [price of melons] gone up suddenly? There is a store round the corner. They sell theirs for five pounds. Transcript B, Nicosia /73

It was sometimes necessary to briefly step out of the role-playing situation to calm children down and prevent disagreements between them from escalating.[2]

The activities chosen for the study are listed below. Each activity is numbered to help identify it.

	Theme
Activity 1	Setting up stores in Cyprus and England. Selling melons (Transcript A)
Activity 2	Running rival stores by buying from a wholesaler. Children to make a profit of £200 with the £100 they were given to sell melons. (Transcript B)
Activity 3	Two rival truck companies, one in Cyprus and the other in England. (Transcript C)
Activity 4	Establishing a bilingual newspaper for readers in England and Cyprus. (Transcript D)

Each activity had an aim and specific objectives:

Activity 1: Setting up stores in Cyprus and England
Aim: to enable conceptual areas to develop through interactive collaborative group contexts.

The children were required to

■ negotiate roles within their stores

■ work out prices for their items

■ develop a system for arranging to import melons more cheaply.

Activity 2: Making a profit
Aim: to enable children to explore the factors affecting profit in the context of store transactions

The objectives were to

■ provide further opportunities to develop understanding of economic concepts such as money, work, cost and buying through store transactions

- encourage children to think about different ideas for selling their items

- encourage children to understand that the selling process involves a degree of competition between stores

- encourage collaboration in fulfilling the demands of the tasks.

Activity 3: Running a trucking company
Aim: To explore the concept of profit further by thinking of related measures to make a company successful.

The objectives were to

- facilitate further collaboration between children by presenting a more demanding task such as setting up rival companies

- use their experiences and skills of negotiation more freely to establish initiatives that would make their companies more successful

- use Turkish and English freely and interchangeably during transactions.

Activity 4: Establishing a bilingual paper
Aim: to explore issues around publishing a newspaper in two languages.

The objectives were to

- understand the purpose of publishing news relevant to readers in Cyprus and England

- to recognise the benefits of group collaboration to produce a newspaper that covered a range of interests

- use the two languages even more interchangeably and naturally during interactions.

Each transcript is identified by a three-digit number system. The first number identifies the chapter dealing with the conceptual area. The second number refers to the possible areas of interpretation by the children of that conceptual area and the third refers to its sequence of recording, hence 4.1.1 tells us that we are in chapter 4, dealing with the first conceptual area (*cost*), looking at the *first* section of cost and the transcript of that first recording. The last point is important as it helps trace the children's thinking and possible areas of development in that thinking. For example, in the first extract in buying, some children may appear to be struggling to understand the relationship between goods and money. This should not be seen as a lack of development in children's thinking but as the beginning of a process that could lead to other areas of development. Because space is limited, I present one or two examples relating to each of the sections of the conceptual areas. At other times I refer to transcripts not shown here but which can be found in the appendix.

COST
The first conceptual area looked at was cost. I was intrigued by the sophistication of some children's thinking. They had various interpretations of what 'cost' might mean.

■ cost as the selling price: children's use of the concept is analysed in terms of their setting the prices of goods for their customers

■ cost as a variable within a transaction: how children changed the prices of items, in response to changing circumstances in their stores

■ cost as fixed or non-negotiable within a transaction: situations when children take uncompromising positions on their set prices

There are examples from each of these areas below and a summary of findings for each area.

1: Setting the price for customers: the Selling Price
This section looks at the price the storekeepers 'set' for their customers. The first extract is from Transcript A, in the Nicosia store, where three storekeepers are discussing the prices they should set for some items they hope to sell in their store.

They ask for each other's views about the prices for items.

Binnur and Funda (7) repeat Şefik's earlier suggested price for an item.

Şefik's utterance in Turkish (8) followed an earlier prompt from Funda reminding people to speak Turkish. Şefik's compliance indicates that he wants to play the game so observed the 'rules' that is, speaking Turkish. Binnur and Funda's repetition suggests that they themselves were observing this rule.

Extract 4.1.1

6	Şefik	(Showing an item)	This is ten pounds.	
7	Binnur	(repeating after Şefik)	*On lira.*	Ten pounds.
	Funda	(prompting Şefik)	*Talk Turkish!*	
8	Şefik	(to others)	*Al!*	Take it!
9	Funda	(showing another item)	*Kaç paradır?*	How much is it?
10	Şefik		*Bir peni.*	One penny.

Transcript A (Nicosia Store) 6-10: (Birsen, Funda, Şefik)

Funda's next utterance (9) sets the conversation in Turkish. Şefik's response (10) confirms the shared understanding that children are willing to play the game of asking/setting prices for items in Turkish. *Kaç paradır?* is a common question asked by a Turkish customer about an item they intend to purchase. Here children use it to determine the prices for items they are selling. In the context of a store we would expect storekeepers to ask each other: *bu kaç para olsun?* [literal translation: how much (money) should this be?] or *bunu kaç para yapalım?* [how much (money) shall we make this?]. The children's responses suggests that there was a common understanding relating to the task at hand of setting prices for items so they were able to negotiate the task without using of complete sentences.

In this extract we see children establishing the rules of their game of fixing prices for items to be sold to customers. Children sought one another's opinion on prices and got varying responses. Agreeing the final price reflects a common agreement between the storekeepers. These children were apparently not too happy about fixing the prices suggested by the first speaker. Turkish is the medium through which such exchanges take place, and in this extract children used *kaç para?*, the Turkish form of the question *how much?* to help determine the price of items.

The following extract was transcribed approximately eighteen months later and reveals some changes that seem to be taking place in the children's thinking about cost. The extract is from Transcript C. In this role-play, children were asked to set up a truck company to transport goods between England and Cyprus. A customer (myself in role) wants them to transport 3000 melons from Cyprus. The children are discussing details of the cost for transporting them.

In this discussion Banu initially asked how much they should charge for transporting melons to Cyprus, saying Banu uses *to* instead of *from* by mistake (146). Banu's request appeared to be understood by the others as it prompted discussions on possible prices to be charged. The figures were discussed in Turkish (148,

---

Extract 4.1.4

142	Banu		Let's look at the prices.	
143	Binnur		*Şimdi !*	Now!
144	Banu		Make some money. I will make some money.	
145	Binnur		Make some ten-pound notes.	
146	Banu		I know. How much to Cyprus?	
147	Binnur		One thousand because three thousand karpuz.	melons
148	Funda		*No! dokuzyüz!*	Nine hundred!
149	Binnur		*No! Sekizyüzelli!*	Eight hundred and fifty!
150	Banu		It's too much. I mean too much watermelons.	
151	Binnur		One thousand No! One thousand five hundred. It depends on the thing. On the way it's a lot of things we will have a price one thousand. If just luggage we will have about five hundred.	
152	Banu	(writing down what is being said)	Hold on a minute...Luggage.	

Transcript C: 142-152 Binnur, Banu, Funda

149), this time without my presence as a customer, whereas on previous occasions it seemed to require my presence to prompt talking in Turkish.

Binnur (151) then appeared to switch to English, possibly because he could not remember the Turkish word for 'thousand', *bin*.

The children – mainly Banu and Binnur – seemed aware that a price would depend on certain variables, such as the kind of items to be transported. Some children thought about carrying other items besides melons, and both Banu and Binnur suggested that the price to be charged would depend on whether they did so. Banu also said that the quantity to be carried also made a difference: that is, transporting three thousand melons would cost more than transporting two thousand (150).

Binnur apparently knew that the distance between Cyprus and England was fixed and would be the major factor determining price. She indicated that the price would depend also on what was to be transported, what kind of goods. Binnur suggests a way forward (151) and Banu agrees and writes down the price (152).

Binnur and Banu both showed some understanding of the notions of cost, and the many factors that contribute to it. It was difficult to assess Funda's thinking on the matter as she made little contribution to this discussion. Her silence could mean she agreed with the arrangements.

During the course of eighteen months, four extracts in all were taken from the activities in Transcripts A, B and C that related to the first example of cost I have presented the first and last ones here. Some of the changes observed in the children's thinking may be related to their new experiences at home or school or perhaps the children moved on to a new stage of development in their thinking and reasoning. All the activities required them to discuss the prices for certain items and services they were to provide for their customers. In the preceding extracts (as seen in extract 4.1.1 above) this was deciding the prices for the items to be sold in the stores. In the fourth extract (4.1.4) this was fixing a price to transport goods from Cyprus.

The children's conversations were not only about exploring the variables of price. They also illustrate how they use two languages interchangeably, borrowing words from English to replace the

Extract 4.2.1

167	Researcher		*Evet..bir tane karpuz istiyorum.*	Yes I would like a melon please.
			Kaç para bu karpuz Türk lirası?	How much is this in Turkish Lira?
			Aman! çok ağır bu karpuz. Yardım et kızım koyayım içine.	These are really heavy. Can you please help me to put them in the bag?
168	Funda		*Beş lira.*	Five pounds.
169	Researcher		*Türk parası mı? Çok ucuz.*	Is it Turkish lira? That's really cheap.
170	Funda	(changing her mind)	*On beş lira.*	Fifteen pounds.
171	Researcher		*O da az para ama.*	That also sounds too cheap but..
172	Funda		*Mahsus yaparık müşteri gelsin diye.*	We are doing it on purpose to make customers come here.
173	Researcher		*Bu prawn cock-tail'ler kaç paradır?*	How much are these Prawn Cocktails?
174	Funda		*On bin idi indirdik sekize.*	It was ten thousand we brought it down to eight (thousand).
175	Researcher		*Peki, niye bu* beef flavoured crisps *iki bin de* prawn cocktail *'ler sekiz?*	Why are these beef flavoured crisps two thousand and the Prawn Cocktails eight?
176	Emine	(pointing at crisps)	*Çünkü bu ondan daha sert.*	Because this is harder than that one.
177	Funda		*Bu eski..hmm.. bu çoktan gelmiş ama hiçbiri almadı.*	These are old.. hmm. They came long time ago but no one bought it!

Extract 4.2.1 (continued)

| 178 | Researcher | *Onun için mi daha ucuza verdiniz?* | Is that why you gave them away cheaper? |
| 179 | Funda | *Evet, Çünkü çok güzeldir.* | Yes because they are really nice. |

Transcript A (Nicosia Store): 167-179: Researcher, Emine, Funda

---

Turkish words they cannot remember. While in previous activities my presence may have prompted the children to speak Turkish (as I sometimes initiated discussions in Turkish) this was not the case here. Children freely borrowed from as well as switching between their languages. The implications of these findings for children's thinking are discussed in more detail in the concluding chapter. We move now to the second example of children's interpretation of cost.

2: Price as a variable within a transaction

This section reveals where children change the price for an item in light of certain factors concerning a transaction. The first extract is from Transcript A, where a customer (myself in role) visits the store and asks about the price of various items.

Despite earlier efforts to determine the prices of items, Emine and Funda do not appear to be in agreement. In this conversation, entirely in Turkish, Emine answers *beş lira* (five pounds) when the customer asks the price of a melon. When the customer expresses surprise at how cheap this is she immediately trebles the price to *on beş lira*. Funda promptly claims that the cheap price was a deliberate attempt to attract customers (172). This was backed by offering the customer a lower price. When I ask about the difference in price for prawn cocktails and beef flavoured crisps (175), Emine replies that items which are in a store longer become the hardest to sell and are therefore sold off cheaply (176).

Funda's response at (174) indicates her awareness that there is a connection between the cost of an item and the time it remains in the store. Her explanation is very like how a Turkish storekeeper would explain a reduction in price. He/she would use *düşürdük* (dropped), instead of *indirdik* (brought down), to imply a reduction in price. Funda's comment indicates her knowledge of the storekeepers' terminology[3] and her good Turkish language skills.

Funda is also aware that it is not good practice for storekeepers to point out that their stock may be *old*. She quickly realises her mistake and cleverly adds that they came 'a few days ago'. Funda may have picked up some of the strategies her parents use in their family store.[4] She tells her customer that she is going to give him one from the *newly arrived ones*. The customer is always made to feel special – the *not so fresh ones* are always meant to be for other customers.

Here we see how children alter the price a customer is charged, although earlier conversations had suggested that they regarded prices as fixed. This conversation between customer and storekeepers shows that they are prepared to change prices according to circumstances. They seem clear that the aim of the storekeeper is to make money and that this means attracting customers to their stores and ensuring that they buy something. If the customer finds the price too high, this is thought to be a good reason for reducing it. But the initial low prices fixed by the store could also have been the result of the storekeepers' lack of knowledge of costs as expressed in Turkish *lira*.[5] The children explain that they will lower prices for items not too fresh and reconsider prices customers think too high which suggests that children are aware of the need not just to attract customers but also to keep them.

The next extract is from Transcript B in the Nicosia store. On this occasion the two stores were competing with each other. Each had to make a certain sum of money within a given period and the store that raised the money first would be the winner. The storekeepers in the first store had been wondering why they were not having much luck with the sale of their new item, pineapples, and then a customer informs them that these prices are higher than in the other store.

Binnur tells the others they need to buy more pineapples (134). Her reason could be that buying greater quantities would mean they could afford to sell them cheaper. But the storekeepers seem to have overlooked the fact that they would need more money to buy them from the wholesaler. If so, it is also possible that an obsession to drive rivals out of business could be the overriding factor in the competition with the other store.[6] But another ex-

Extract 4.2.2

129	Researcher		*Ananas var mı?*	Are there any pineapples?
130	Funda		*Evet iki tane var.*	Yes there are two.
131	Researcher		*Kusura bakmayın almayacağım çünkü diğer dükkanda bir liraya satıyorlar.*	I am sorry I won't buy it because they sell it for one pound in the other store.
			On tane için yirmi lira vereceğim size ama onda on liraya.	I give you twenty pounds for ten of them but the other store sells them for only ten.
132	Binnur	(to Göksel)	How much did he say they are selling?	
133	Göksel		One pound.	
134	Binnur		We got to get pineapples. Everybody need to get pineapples!	
135	Göksel	(shouts for customers)	Pineapples are one pound!	
136	Funda	(to Şefik)	Go away!	
137	Sefik		I am a customer!	
138	Funda		Shall I make more pineapples?	
138	Birsen		Yes. Make two more	

Transcript B (Nicosia Store): 129-139 Binnur, Şefik, Funda

planation is that Binnur could not encompass all the relevant factors affecting the running of a store.

So the price of pineapples was halved by Nicosia store to one pound. Again, the other two storekeepers Funda and Şefik seem not to have responded to Binnur's suggestion. Possibly the children were becoming accustomed to working with each other and were developing a sense of understanding each other's intentions. Compared to Transcript A, we see fewer confrontational issues and arguments relating to fixing prices. In Transcript B suggestions are still being made about fixing prices, but this appears to be less of an issue than in other contexts (see extracts 4.2.4/4.3.2/4.3.3). The decision to reduce the price was accepted without much discussion.

The other possibility is that the children were losing interest in the game, but this would not explain the enthusiasm shown in the exchanges, nor the passion with which they put forward suggestions.

Two important trends are revealed in this extract. Firstly, once they discovered why they were not selling enough pineapples, the children opted for larger quantities so they could sell them more cheaply. Their assumption appeared to be that if they had more items they could sell them more cheaply, because they had more to sell and that this would enable the store to make the sum of money needed to win the competition. Secondly, they were reacting to the lack of customers. We will see that when a storekeeper was given the choice to change prices when there were many customers, he decided not to do so. This showed his confidence that they would still sell their products, even at a high price. In the activity discussed above, the children felt they had no choice but to lower their prices because they had no customers. They were also aware that the other store was selling the same product more cheaply. Competition from another store was tolerated but only so long as sufficient customers bought things from *their* store. Once the customers stopped coming, the burden of competition was really felt, and led to drastic action.

In this section I have tried to show that children's development of the concept of price *can* be variable. Children appeared to show various kinds of understanding about fixing prices and this, I argue, is linked to their cultural experiences, the nature of the activities organised and the way children interpreted the activities and interacted with one another. Children's perceptions influenced their interactions with others around them. This in turn demonstrated the important role played by language in communication and the interpretation of learning environments. A bilingual medium of interaction affected the process of development positively, as it enabled children to view activities through two equally useful mediums.

The final two extracts are from the third example of children's interpretation of cost.

3 Price as fixed within a transaction

In these examples, the price has been firmly established and fixed in a transaction. The first extract is from Transcript B, in the Nicosia store, where once again I act as a customer visiting the store, asking about the price changes.

Extract 4.3.1

71	Researcher		*Ben geçen hafta gelmiştim, bana büyük sattınız.*	I came last week. You sold me big ones.
72	Funda	(anticipating the complaint)	*E...Birazcık çıktı parası*	Ehm. The price has gone up a bit.
73	Researcher		*Niye böyle ansızın yükselttiniz?*	Why have you raised it suddenly?
			Diğer tarafta bir dükkan var, onlar büyükleri beş pound'a satıyorlar.	There is a store on the other side, they sell theirs for five pounds.
74	Binnur		*E..biraz para lâzım.*	Ehm. We need some money.
75	Researcher		*Fazla almayacağım çünkü bende de para yok.*	I won't be able to buy a lot because I haven't got any money.
76	Funda		Twenty four pounds.	
77	Researcher		Two small ones, are they two pounds each?	
78	Göksel		Yes.	
79	Researcher		I will have two small ones please.	

Extract 4.3.1 continued

80	Binnur		The big ones are twenty four and small ones. That will be thirty pounds.	
81	Funda	(sees an approaching customer)	Hello! What would you like?	
82	Sefik		How much are these?	
83	Funda		These? Three pounds.	
		(takes the money)		
84	Sefik	(large melon)	How much are these?	
85	Funda	Five pounds.		
86	Researcher		*Teşekkür ederim..* *İyi işler.*	Thank you. Good sales!
87	Banu	(small melon)	How much is that again?	
88	Binnur/Funda		Three pounds.	

Transcript B (Nicosia Store): 71-88 Funda, Göksel, Binnur, Şefik, Researcher

Funda (72) anticipates the complaint indicates that the price 'has gone up a bit'. This refers to the price of melons, and she explains the reason for this in Turkish (74).[7]

During the continuing discussion on buying and selling (75-88), the storekeepers implement their agreement on prices without further discussion. This is also shown by their precise calculation of totals payable by the customers – small melons at three pounds, larger ones at six – as well as the change given to the customers.

After this exchange, the children in the store count their takings and realise that they are only five pounds short of their target. Funda points out that they need five more pounds to reach two hundred pounds. When the next customer arrives and asks the price for big melons, the three storekeepers unanimously declare a new price of five pounds, without any prior discussion. All made the decision at the same time and informed the customer. Their satisfaction is evident when they declare their 'victory' over Cappodocia:

Hey! We beat you guys! (Transcript B, Nicosia Store: 1/97).

Up to this point, however, the storekeepers decide not to lower a price they raised previously despite complaints from a customer. The storekeepers knew they needed to raise more money to meet the competition from the other store, so they stuck to their original plan and kept their prices high. The storekeepers were also aware of the presence of other customers, which increased their chances for making a sale. Despite the complaints, the outcome justified their decision not to lower their prices, and their earlier predictions made for sales at the new price.

In the next extract from Transcript C, a customer (myself in role) wants his melons to be transported from Cyprus and is negotiating a price from the company, set up in England. The children are now running a transport company not a store.

Extract 4.3.6

158	Researcher	Yes the same person.. Yalnız şey oldu. Benim arkadaşım Kıbrısta sizin diğer branch'ınıza gitmiş ve sizin arkadaşlarınızla konuşmuş, Onlar sizi arıyabilirler yakında	My friend in Cyprus went and spoke to the people at your branch. They may contact you soon.
		Bana fiatları verebilecekmisiniz?	Will you be able to give me the prices?
159	Banu	Bin lira.	A thousand pounds.
160	Researcher	Bin mi?	One thousand?
161	Banu	Çok uzun yol	It is really a long way.

Extract 4.3.6 (continued)

162	Researcher		*Kaç gün alacak..*	How long will it take.
163	Funda		*Dört gün.*	Four days.
164	Researcher		*Tamam. Ama başka kumpanya bana dokuzyüz lira demişti.*	Alright, but another company has told me nine hundred pounds.
			Zaman ayni idi ama fiyat daha ucuz idi.	The time was the same but the price was cheaper.
165	Binnur		*Bir dakka.*	One minute.
166	Göksel	(to researcher)	Hello!	
167	Banu	(to researcher)	*Şey! Adınız?*	Your name?
		(phoning Cyprus)	*Tözün beyin arkadaşı gelmiş size. Siz dokuzyüz liraya getireceğiniz demişsiniz, Siz yanlış mı yaptınız?*	Mr. Tözün's friend has come to you and said that you have told him you could bring them here for nine hundred. Did you make a mistake?
168	Göksel		*O zaman bin lira olsun.*	In that case let it be thousand pounds.
169	Banu	(finalising her conversation on the phone, turns to the researcher)	*Evet, tamam. Siz yanlış hesapladınız.*	Yes, alright! You did the wrong calculation.

Extract 4.3.6 (continued)

170	Researcher		*Pardon bana başka kumpanya o fiatı vermişti, sizinkiler değil!*	Sorry, it was another company who gave me that price, not yours!
171	Funda	(confirming with other Storekeepers)	*Sekizyüzellidokuz.*	Eight hundred and fifty nine!
172	Researcher		*O zaman ben kabul ediyorum.*	In that case I accept.
173	Binnur	(to the researcher)	*Siz dört gün içinde gelin.*	You come and see us in four days.

Transcript C: 158-173 (Funda, Göksel, Binnur, Researcher)

As a customer I am quoted one thousand pounds to have my melons transported from Cyprus (159). I want to cause a bit of a stir so I tell them the other company – based in Cyprus – has quoted me nine hundred pounds for the same job.

Banu phones Cyprus and explains the situation in Turkish to the company director there. Her explanation appears to indicate that the price of one thousand pounds between the two companies was actually fixed and that they have agreed on it. Banu's query following the customer's complaint suggests that she was trying to clear the misunderstanding on to the agreed price with the company in Cyprus (169).

When the directors in Cyprus deny such a claim, it becomes evident that it was I who was causing a problem over the price and that the children have agreed on the fixed prices and stuck to their agreement.

Göksel's response as a director in Cyprus (170) indicates that he may have forgotten what had been agreed. Banu's call also served as a useful reminder of the agreed price between the two branches. Banu tells the customer that he must have made the wrong calculation (171).

Much as in Sections 2 and 3, the extract appears to demonstrate children's – Banu's in this case – increasing understanding about fixing a price. As the initiative of one storekeeper shows, even a crafty customer could not succeed in getting a lower price for himself. While rejecting an attempt to undermine fixed prices, their willingness to negotiate a reduction in the face of a genuine alternative offer appears to support this point. Although it was not possible to prove that all the children had the same level of understanding at all times, the total of seven extracts which were analysed in this section all showed a degree of sophistication in the children's thinking about fixing prices.

Summary on the concept of cost

The three sections analysed show a progression in the children's thinking about costs due to a several factors.

In Section 1 we saw children engaged in fixing prices for items in their store. There appeared to be little disagreement, partly because the children were unfamiliar with the activities and their customers did not challenge the prices. Although the children talked to each other, there seemed to be little interactive debate. There did appear to be an agreed framework for pricing items, however. The children informed each other of their intended pricing and this became accepted within the group. Even Göksel, who was constantly undermined by the girls, was allowed to put forward his suggestion (see Transcript A, Cappodocia in the appendix). The two girls in particular, Banu and Emine, collaborated well and this appeared to indicate more than just being friends. They had good ideas about pricing items and these were close to actual prices. Emine even agreed with Göksel because she believed that the price he suggested was close to the item sold in the cinema (see Transcript A, Cappodocia: 95 in the appendix).

As the activities became more challenging they acted as catalysts for increased interaction. The decisions relating to fixing price appeared to be influenced by ongoing competition and/or complaining customers. Reluctance to change prices was most evident when the competition from the other store was minimal or non-existent. These examples indicate that the children were able to take account of more than one factor when fixing price. As the activities progressed, they became increasingly sophisticated about how changes in prices affected their sales.

The specific role-playing contexts facilitated such thinking. Section 2 provides useful examples of how, according to Kourilisky and Graff (1985), planned instruction can enhance children's learning of economic concepts.

The children's discussions about whether to raise or lower the prices, or whether to buy more melons provide evidence of children's thinking. Their ideas about how to price certain items were shaped by their past experiences from home or another country – Turkey, Cyprus, and Germany.

The children told the complaining customers why they thought some items were more expensive than others. Their apparent unwillingness to provide explanations to each other during fixing prices may also be related to wider interpersonal relationships.[8] However, there were also examples of children communicating their reasons and ideas for prices and clearly justifying these to each other (Extract 4.1.4). This may also be a development in their thinking, in that children only felt an obligation to justify their prices to outsiders during the initial activities [that is, complaining customers (4.2.1)] whereas in later activities they began to explain things to each other (extract 4.1.4). I looked at Francis' (1998) analysis of children's construction of gender discourses during interactions.

Children did not openly use the words 'cost' or 'profit' in their discussions. Instead they said 'price' to imply transactions related to cost or any other relevant activities. Interestingly the word *fiyat* used during the interactions is the Turkish word for *price* and carries the same dictionary meaning: *the price paid or charged for something.*

These bilingual children were sensitive to the use of Turkish in specific situations, such as during their interactions with me. My findings here are supported by Baker (2001), who notes bilingual pupils' superior ability to monolinguals in communicative sensitivity. The increased use of Turkish by the children as the activities progressed supports this point. Children made decisions about when to use Turkish and continued using it even when I was not there.

This section has drawn attention to the role of language as a tool for transmitting culturally acquired concepts in a collaborative oral medium. Vygotsky (1962) suggests that children's conceptual development is to be perceived in the context of such a tool, through which concepts are to be negotiated. My findings assume that an increase in the frequency of using Turkish was a manifestation of the children's thinking processes. The bilingual medium enables such processes to take place in a richer linguistic environment, not simply because of different linguistic devices, but because of the richness of experiences transmitted through each language. I have tried to illustrate how such ideas were expressed as words and sentences and transferred between the two languages. Cummins' (1977, 1980) Common Underlying Proficiency Model gives us insights into this theory of bilingual competence.

My findings support my claim that children do not appear to follow universal stages of development. These examples show that some children were more sophisticated about one area that arose in fixing prices than they were in others. For example, Şefik appeared to depend mainly on the other storekeepers to fix prices, but took a leading role in the bilingual newspaper activity, suggesting how different sections of the newspaper should be organised. Similarly it was interesting that some of the children who had first hand experiences of family stores showed understanding of the uses of money beyond mere exchange.[9] These children seemed unsure of the comparative prices for items during price fixing. Bearing in mind the age and maturity argument put forward by Burris (1983), Goldstein and Oldham (1979) and Furth (1980), children in this study do not appear to be going through the same stages at the same time when acquiring economic concepts. Such a development occurs at different levels for each aspect of the conceptual area for each child, but this does not prove or disprove the validity of the stage-theory argument.[10] It merely shows that children's development should not be analysed solely from that perspective.

I have shown that children's understanding of fixing prices in role playing store contexts was affected by a number of factors. I constantly needed to remind myself that patterns that emerge in one activity would not necessarily surface in another. As this was indeed the case, we can conclude that the factors vary, depending on the situation and the children's own experiences.

In the next chapter I explore my findings under the second conceptual area, money.

Notes

1 Children were developing strategies of how they would interact with others and attract them as customers or even spy on them to see how much they were selling their melons for and to sell their melons.

2 Some children adapted to role-playing situations earlier than others, so coming back 'into play' after each period between transcripts was relatively easier for them. For others this took longer.

3 Her parents own a grocery store

4 It is quite a common practice for Turkish customers to have similar conversation with the storekeepers, asking the details about each of the food products before buying them, a ritual common to many stores in Turkey, Cyprus and Turkish stores in England.

5 This may suggest that children were not sure of the conversion rate between the two currencies, sterling and the Turkish lira.

6 Examples of this sort are not too hard to find among real life store situations in Turkey and Cyprus.

7 Remember that in Transcript B, (extract 5.2.3) a competition was set up between the stores to encourage storekeepers to use their initiative. Funda's response appears to refer to this.

8 Some boys did not get on well with girls therefore girls may not have felt any need to explain themselves to boys and visa versa. Equally this may be assumed to be the case for 'friends' working together, not justifying their decisions to each other.

9 Sharing real life examples of people working in their parents' stores as musicians or buying stock from the card stockist. Children appeared to be aware that money was used in those situations.

10 Piaget also emphasised the need for children to have a variety of experiences in order to progress 'naturally' through the stages.

5

Children's understanding of money

Having shown how children's thinking about cost develops, we now examine children's understandings about money. I observed children's interpretations of money as:

- a medium of exchange, that is, as a necessary tool in the reciprocity of a transaction – here in the context of store transactions, and

- as represented by the currencies used in different countries – how children understand Turkish lira and sterling and their comparative value.

1 Money as used in reciprocal transactions

Two extracts provide examples: the first is from Transcript A in Nicosia store. The storekeepers are busily putting names and price labels on their goods before being told they are about to be visited by customers.

Here the conversations are primarily in Turkish. Funda's announcement (85) and the response of the others indicate the children's willingness to play the game. The storekeepers are busy getting their shops ready for the customers. Şefik's comments about *paraları* (the money) concern making paper for money for transactions (80).

Extract 5.1.1

85	Funda	(to others)	*İşte geldiler*	Here they come
86	Şefik		You have to speak Turkish. They don't know Turkish.	
87	Birsen	(to Şefik)	*konuşma*	Don't talk!
88	Funda	(with excitement)	*Geldi! Geliyor!*	They are here! They are nearly here!
89	Şefik	(to others)	*Paraları yapalım.*	Let's make the money.
90	Funda	(to others)	*Geliyor be çabuk !*	Hurry up, they're coming!
91	Şefik		*Paraları yaptım, paraları yaptım!*	I done the money, I done the money!
92	Funda		They are coming	
93	Binnur		Hurry up!	
94	Şefik	(Showing the money!)	*Bak,! on bin, üç bin, dört bin*	Look! Ten thousand, three thousand, four thousand.

Transcript A (Nicosia Store): 89-94 Şefik, Funda, Binnur

This short extract shows children's awareness of money as important to facilitate the functioning of their stores.

The next extract is also from Transcript A, in Cappodocia store. The storekeepers are also preparing for customers and producing 'money'.

Göksel's proposition (293) is unclear. He might be asking Banu to make price labels to display on the melons or paper money to be used in the transaction.. Banu's response (294) suggests the latter, indicating a functional role for the money to be used in the transactions. Her suggestion for the inclusion of pence as well as pounds indicates her awareness of English as well as the complexities of fixing price, and that prices can be in pounds or in pounds and pence. Banu (298) urges fellow storekeepers to make more money to be used for transactions in their store.

Extract 5.1.2

293	Göksel	(to others)	Hey! Make some money for the melons!
294	Banu		We always make pounds why don't we make pence?
295	Göksel	(to others)	Make some money for the melons. Twenty p. yes. Melons! Fifty pounds?
296	Banu		Yeah! There is.
297	Göksel		What's gonna be fifty pounds?
298	Banu		Some money, some money!
299	Emine		Talk English!

Transcript A (Cappodocia Store): 293- 299 Banu, Göksel, Emine

Clearly the children were aware that money has a role in reciprocal transactions in a store. Although not directly questioned about what they thought the purposes of money were, their preparations suggest that they saw it as necessary for buying and selling in their stores. The children's ideas about money appear to be reinforced by collaborative activities. Their thinking seems to be based on accumulation of their personal and cultural experiences, as well as being part of their natural development as they grow older. Culture is also a factor – as Vygotsky (1962) argued, children use their language as a tool to transmit their cultural experiences. It is the way these cultural values are accumulated that is explored in my study. Wertsch (1985), however, criticises Vygotsky for perceiving culture as a universally produced and transmitted set of value systems.

2. Money as representing currencies used in different countries

The activities set for the children were designed to explore their perceptions of processes of transaction in Cyprus, Turkey and England, and the different currencies representing the value of the items bought and sold.

The first example is from Transcript A in Cappodocia store.

The storekeepers finalised their price labels and the money to be used for sales, sterling as well as Turkish lira. Customers visit their store.

Extract 5.2.1

220	Binnur		I get everything, there is hardly anything in their store ... Ah! Coca Cola!
221	Göksel	(to Binnur)	Let's go!
222	Binnur		Ten pounds, eleven pounds. What?
223	Göksel		Yes. That's what I have been saying.
224	Binnur		Fifteen, sixteen.
225	Banu	(to Göksel)	Before you take that money Mr!
226	Göksel	(referring to the note he is holding)	It doesn't worth all that much in English money.
227	Banu	(to Göksel)	Before you take that money could you...It's weird!
228	Binnur		It's not the same money around.
229	Funda	(pointing at the note Göksel is holding)	Excuse me! That money looks a bit weird to me.

Transcript A (Cappodocia Store): 220- 229 Göksel, Banu, Funda, Binnur

---

In this extract the storekeepers are responding to Göksel, who takes the 'weird' looking money from their store. The customers are apparently aware that the money is Turkish lira despite re-marking that it 'looks a bit weird'(229). The storekeepers also comment on its appearance while they are making it (227). Except for Göksel it is unclear what the children think about the relation-ship in value between the two currencies (226).

This extract is an example of the children's interactions and their comments on the 'new' currency. Although all the children have visited Turkey and North Cyprus – which both use Turkish cur-rency – only one commented on the relative value of Turkish lira and sterling. The children did not comment on the value of the Turkish money they made, perhaps because they kept saying it looked 'weird' or perhaps because they do not know the comparative values of the two currencies. Children's experiences in Turkey and Cyprus may not have exposed them to local stores, especially since most visits are in summer so they spend their time on the beach.

The next example is from Transcript A in the first store. Here a customer (myself in role) visits the store in Cyprus and inquires about the prices for prawn cocktail crisps.

Extract 5.2.2

156	Researcher		*Merhaba! Bu dükkan yeni açıldı galiba.*	Hello! It looks as if this is a newly opened store.
			Prawn Cocktail 'ler kaç para?	How much are the prawn cocktails?
157	Funda	(together)	*Sekiz Lira.*	Eight pounds.
	Binnur			
158	Researcher		*Türk Lirası mı?*	In Turkish pounds?
159	Funda		*Nasıl olursa.*	How ever you like.
	Binnur			
160	Researcher		*Demek siz burda İngiliz lirası da alırsınız?*	So you take English pounds as well do you?
161	Funda		*Evet.*	Yes.
	Binnur			
162	Researcher		*Peki ne vereyim ben size?* Kaç Türk Lirası?	Ok! What shall I give you? How much Turkish Lira?
163	Binnur		*Dört bin.*	Four thousand
164	Funda		*Hayır altı bin!*	No! six thousand.

Extract 5.2.2 (continued)

165	Researcher		Altı bin mi? Tamam.Size on bin veriyorum. Bana üstünü verin lutfen!	Six thousand? OK!I am giving you ten thousand. Can I have the change please?
166	Funda		Başka birşey istiyor musunuz?	Would you like anything else?
167	Researcher		Evet. Bir tane karpuz istiyorum.	Yes. I would like a melon please.
			Kaç para bu?	How much is it?
168	Funda		Beş lira.	Five pounds.
169	Researcher		Türk Lirasi mı?	Is that in Turkish lira?
170	Funda	(a pause)	On beş lira.	Fifteen pounds.
171	Researcher		O da az geldi ama..	That doesn't sound much either but..
172	Funda		Mahsus yaparık müşteri gelsin diye.	We are doing it on purpose to attract customers.
173	Researcher	(pretending)	Bu Prawn Cocktail´ ler kaç paraydılar, on bin ..yoksa?	How much were these prawn cocktails again? Was it ten thousand, or..?
174	Funda		On bin idi sekize indirdik aşağıya.	It was ten thousand but we dropped it down to eight.

Transcript A (Nicosia Store): 156-174 Researcher, Funda, Binnur, Banu

The example above does not indicate that the children understand the comparative value of the two currencies. This is true also of Funda, the most verbal of all the storekeepers. When asked the price of pineapples (157) and questioned on the price she has named (158), her answer indicates that she has little idea of the exchange rate and other of her responses also support this view (168,170,174).

Children's use of Turkish in their conversations enabled me to explore whether there were correlations between their ideas and knowledge about sterling and Turkish lira, and their experiences. I also had the chance to talk to them before and after some of the activities. These exchanges suggest that despite visiting Cyprus and Turkey, most of the children were unfamiliar with the relative value of the currencies. Children's observations on the physical differences in the notes and coins appeared to suggest that perhaps their understanding was limited only to how they looked.

Because the children only visited Turkey or Cyprus during the holiday season, their experience with money was confined to buying things with Turkish lira, rather than comparing the two exchange rates – unless they compared it with how much they paid for a similar item in the UK. Few shops use Turkish lira and sterling in Cyprus or Turkey. Generally, when children were speaking in 'thousands' they meant Turkish lira and 'five pounds' meant sterling. I found no evidence that anyone but Göksel understood the relative values of sterling and Turkish lira.

Several points arise. Firstly, children appear to need a variety of stimuli to develop conceptually. In his study of children's perceptions of capital, Ross summarises this well:

> But I would suggest that the experience is not properly conceptualised until a further stimulus is applied: more information about the industries, the chance to engage in conversation about setting up a business or discussing a picture of a workplace. They both seem to be necessary conditions for conceptual development, though neither on their own could be a sufficient condition. (Ross, 1992, p 115)

Ross concluded that children needed to have background data information about capital. For Ross, 'data' are the actual information for children: the media, parents' conversations and so on. My argument is that children's cultural environment plays an important part in such development. I agree that such experiences need further stimuli, that is contexts of learning as shown in his study. It is clear that the learning contexts created here with money were insufficient to act as stimuli to such development.

Secondly, the notion of culturally acquired concepts needs to be treated with some caution. Having been immersed in particular cultural practices does not naturally lead to the acquisition of related values. Visiting Turkey and Cyprus regularly did not ensure understanding of the relative values of Turkish lira and sterling. Any learning contexts created should ensure that children have first hand experience of conversing and actively participating in relevant discussions. In my conclusion I re-asses the Vygotskian notions of 'parental modelling' and 'transmission' of cultural values, and look more critically at the arguments for development.

Summary

Traditional developmental psychology has had a preoccupation with discovering the 'general laws of developmental change' (Karmiloff-Smith, 1992). There is also an obsession with traditional methods of investigation: namely systematic observation, experimentation and appropriate measurement. Implicit in this approach are assumptions about the 'right' knowledge to be acquired.

This section on money challenges such notions. The methodology used involved open-ended interactive role-playing contexts. Children's naturally occurring discourse has been analysed in relation to a number of situations and games. Activities were designed to encourage children to collaborate in tackling the challenges set. Bilingual exchanges were encouraged, to accelerate the process and possibly to give insights into children's thinking on related conceptual areas.

I have tried to explore the uses of money other than as a medium of exchange. Money has other functions, for example as means of capital accumulation (Sutton, 1962) and as a store of wealth (Ross, 1992). Children do not, as claimed by Burris (1983) and others, go through a 'universal stage' in their development of understanding about money. According to both Sutton and Ross, children's social context of learning, their first hand experiences, are important in their development of a concept. I have argued that children's understanding of a particular concept is influenced by a variety of experiences and have tried in this chapter to illustrate the role of culturally acquired experiences, whether – in line with Vygotsky – acquired individually or socially.

So far we have seen how children's particular cultural experiences may influence their understanding of a particular aspect of a conceptual area. My findings support the view that development is not linear and/or does not necessarily follow a sequence of stages, and also that cultural development or culturally acquired experiences take place at various levels, affecting individual children in different ways.

I have discussed children's understanding of money as a conceptual area and shown how cultural experiences may affect the development of an aspect of that concept. The cultural experiences of the children in my study are in home and community environments, in which Turkish is the predominant language. So their thinking needed to use Turkish as a medium. We saw how they used Turkish as well as English while talking amongst themselves, supporting the argument that bilingual children often transfer ideas between their two languages. The frequency of transfer depends on a variety of factors, for example the contexts of interaction. Their preference for Turkish during the activities indicates transfer between the two languages. The bilingual context made it possible to look at the children's ideas through two different mediums and establish that:

> they used money as a concept in their everyday experiences and that they started school speaking mainly Turkish.

Consequently we can assume that these children's initial experiences of money are likely to have been acquired in Turkish and perhaps developed further in both English and Turkish speaking contexts. One of the difficulties in assessing children's thinking about money was the small size of the sample. One example is worth noting: the children used money as *change* during transactions.

From what they said, the children appeared to be aware that when money was used to pay for something, part of the processes involved was giving change. This indicates an extension in their thinking relating to financial transactions. This is illustrated in this extract from Transcript B in Cappodocia Store.

Here Funda tells the storekeeper what change she should give her in the transaction (55) having, we assume, handed over a ten pound note.

Extract 5.3.1

53	Funda	Can I have two big ones. How much are they?
54	Banu	Four pounds. Altogether they are eight pounds.
55	Funda	Just give me two pounds change. Thank you. I am not going to come to your store again.
56	Şefik	We don't want you here!

Transcript B (Coppodocia Store): 53-56 Funda, Banu, Şefik

In relation to cost we see that children know that items needed to be sold at a higher price than they were bought for and that the children were aware of the role of money in the reciprocal nature of transactions, used money in exchange of goods and services, and showed some understanding of the variables that affect the prices they charge.

The chapter on cost showed that children were aware of the purposes and processes involved in setting the 'right' prices for items in their stores and had useful ideas about what was involved in pricing their items in order to make money. This chapter demonstrates that the children were aware of the role money played in the reciprocal arrangement of store transaction contexts because of their culturally related experiences.

In the next chapter we look at children's thinking as customers.

6

Children's understanding of buying

The third conceptual area to be explored is that of buying. I looked at the children's interpretation of their roles as customers under two main sections:

Buying from a wholesaler: children were given opportunities to buy items from a wholesaler (myself in role). Their ideas on prices, buying and selling are analysed.

Buying from another – rival – store: The children often visited each other's stores as customers and bought items they sold in their own stores. Children's ideas about the prices charged and their responses to each other are analysed.

1 Buying from a wholesaler

I have transcribed a total of five extracts. This section has three transcripts, taken from the five I made. These are the first, second and last, as they provide useful examples of the way the children's thinking developed. The first from Transcript A in Nicosia store, when I, the wholesaler, am approached by a group of prospective buyers. All extracts shown here are set in the context of a competition game organised as part of Activity Two.

The children appear to have little idea about the number of melons they should buy from the wholesaler (16), despite being told the sterling equivalent of the price offered (15). The store-

Extract 6.1.1

11	Researcher		Merhaba, Merhaba. Ben karpuz satıyorum. Karpuz istermisiniz?	Hello, Hello! I sell melons. Would you like some?
12	All		Evet!	Yes!
13	Researcher		Kaça olduğunu soracak mısınız?	Would you like to know how much it is going to cost?
14	All		Evet!	Yes !
15	Researcher		Bir pound karpuz beş bin Türk Lirası vereceğim.	One pound (in weight) is five thousand Turkish Lira.
			Yaklaşık yirmibeş penidir.	This is worth about twenty five pence.
			Kaç tane vereyim?	How many would you like?
16	Binnur Funda		Üç tane	Three of them.
17	Researcher		Sadece üç tane mi?	Just three?
18	Sefik	(whispering to Funda)	Beş, beş!	Five, five
19	Funda		Beş tane.	Five of them.
20	Researcher		Sizin müşterileriniz az galiba.	It looks as if you do not have many customers.
			Tamam ben size vereyim yarın yine gelirim.	OK! I will give you these, I can come tomorrow.
21	Sefik		Yarın birde gel!	Come at one tomorrow!

Transcript B (Coppodocia Store): 11-21 Şefik, Funda, Binnur, Researcher

keepers' apparent hesitation over buying the melons may suggest that they have few customers or they have not decided what price to charge their own customers. The children's apparent ignorance on the relative value of the two currencies, noted in the last chapter, may also have contributed to their uncertainty.

The first extract is from Transcript B in the second store. I play the part of the wholesaler who is approached by a group of prospective customers.

This conversation indicates that the customers have some awareness of the relationship between what is paid to the wholesaler and the price they charge their customers. Şefik's proposal for a price is promptly rejected (10).

Extract 6.1.2

2	Researcher	(Calling out for customers)	*Ucuz karpuz var !* *Ucuz karpuz var !*	Cheap melons! Cheap melons!
		(to Banu)	*Merhaba !*	Hello!
3	Banu		We come to get some melons.	
4	Researcher		*Böyle güzel karpuz gördünüz mü hiç? Tanesi bir lira.*	Have you ever seen such beautiful melons? They are a pound each.
			Kaç tane istiyorsunuz?	How many would you like?
5	Banu		*Iki tane.*	Two of them.
6	Researcher		*Sadece iki tane mi?*	Just two?
		(Banu gives him a ten pound note)	*Tamam! Ben sana sekiz lira vereceğim.*	OK! I will give you eight pounds change.
7	Sefik	(to Banu)	*Kaç tane aldın?*	How many did you buy?
8	Banu		*Iki tane. Şimdi biz bunları nasıl satacağız?*	Two. How are we gonna sell these now?

Extract 6.1.2 (continued)

9	Sefik		*Beş lira!*	Five pounds!
10	Banu	(to Sefik)	*Olmaz pahalı olur! Tanesini bir elli yapalım mı?*	No, it will be too expensive! Shall we make it one-fifty
			Herhalde bunlar yetmez. Sen git daha al!	These will probably be not enough. Go and buy some more!

Transcript B (Cappodocia Store): 2-10 Şefik, Banu, Researcher

Banu is thinking of other variables in attracting customers too and is aware that no storekeeper fixes prices on a whim. The customers may not be able to afford the price asked. Banu's comment (8) appears to indicate that she is alert to the competition from the other store and that they need to think carefully about how many items they buy from the wholesaler. If they buy too many, some may be left unsold in the store. This extract that shows one of the storekeepers – Banu – is aware of these related points when making the deal with the wholesaler, whereas others seem not to have considered such aspects of trade.

The next example is taken from the final extract from Transcript B in the first store. The wholesaler – myself in role – announces that he has pineapples for sale and Funda and Birsen decide to buy some.

The storekeepers appear to have an organised approach to the wholesaler. Binnur and Funda know how many pineapples they need. Their decision on the numbers follows their queries about the price (113, 114). Further evidence that this is a planned approach is shown by Funda's response (119).

Here we see a more coherent approach to buying. Storekeepers Binnur and Funda are aware that there are other points to consider. Their reluctance to use up all their money shows that they are thinking of other uses for it. They know they should limit the number of items they buy at one time so they do not accumulate unsold stock (see extract 6.1.2).

Extract 6.1.5

112	Funda	(to wholesaler)	*Pineapple'lar kaç para?*	How much are the pineapples?
113	Researcher		*Bunlar da bir lira.*	These are one pound as well.
114	Binnur		*Biz beş tane istiyoruz.*	We want five of them.
115	Researcher		*Beş lira lütfen.*	Five pounds please.
116	Binnur	(to Göksel preparing the pineapples)	Don't cut it out, colour it in!	
117	Göksel		I want to colour it in!	
		(Shouting)	We got pineapples!	
118	Researcher		*Çok ananasım var!*	I got plenty more pineapples!
119	Funda	(to wholesaler)	*Biz aldık istemiyoruz başka.*	We got some, we don't need any more.

Transcript B (Nicosia Store): 112-119 Binnur, Göksel, Funda, Researcher

Clearly Binnur and Funda have developed their understanding of buying from a wholesaler and the influence of a variety of factors. The nature of the activity, the children's interactions and the role of the researcher all appear to have played a part in this development. However, it is the children's own interpretations of these activities in relation to their experience that warrants examination.

In this section I have considered the children's thinking in relation to several variables. When the children were buying from a wholesaler they were aware of:

The effect of the prices charged by the wholesaler on

- ■ the prices they would set for their own customers

- ■ the number of items they bought from the wholesaler.

The variables influencing their decisions to buy were:

- ■ how much money they had in hand in their stores

- ■ the number of customers they had

- ■ the nature of the competition

- ■ the wholesaler's prices.

Except for Banu, the initial extracts show little of the children's thinking about buying from a wholesaler. They simply bought items without considering the consequences, so soon found themselves with no money for further purchases. They did not appear to relate the prices they paid to the wholesaler to the prices they fixed in their own stores.

Later transcripts show that the children are beginning to take account of certain variables. Having made hasty buying decisions, they were now thinking of the consequences for the situations in their stores. For example, Funda and Binnur bought twenty melons on the wholesaler's first visit but on the second said that they wished to buy more but were broke. The final extract above shows how when they had already acquired sufficient pineapples, they informed the wholesaler that they had enough and would not need any more.

These findings appear to contradict some of the work of developmental psychologists such as Burris (1983) and Schug and Birkley (1985), who suggest universal development occurs in linear stages. The notion of development is critically analysed by a number of psychologists. Broughton (1987) argues that development is produced by social processes whereas developmental psychologists see development as a 'naturally' produced social process. Social forces act on the individual, who is seen as a passive recipient. Broughton argues:

> Rather than conceiving of social effects on individual development, the very possibility of development and of individuals is premised upon a particular social formation.... The very conditions of possibility of development, as we know and experience it, are constituted by society. (Broughton, 1987, p14)

Broughton's particular 'social formations' are incorporated into the interactive learning contexts created in this study. The informal learning situations created facilitate social interaction within the boundaries of set tasks. Through such interaction and within the context of the set activities, children evaluate the new and discovered information within the context of their existing knowledge.

There is some support for the view that when social activities are created which reflect children's cultural experiences this accelerates children's development. Studies highlight the role of culturally relevant experiences in children's conceptual development, such as seen in Jahoda's (1983) study. In the present case, the learning contexts of role-play trading situations appear to have contributed to children's awareness of the factors involved.

The extracts used here are set in the context of related events – the store competition game was based on the stores competing and making a profit from their sales. The processes of such transactions appear to have advanced the children's thinking on economic areas such as profit. Although there is little detailed evidence of the children's thinking about the competition in the extracts analysed, other sections illustrate children exploring related ideas that have influenced their thinking during this particular game.

The sample extracts show how the children's awareness of all the variables that affect the process of buying from the wholesaler developed and how they became increasingly receptive to the challenges as the activities progressed. Their individual evaluation of the activities may have had this effect, along with conditional factors that influenced their actions, such as the competition. It was not always possible to establish a direct link between specific areas of the children's thinking about the various issues and their actions relating to buying. The verbal interactions provided insufficient evidence on which to base assumptions about their understanding of specific variables, but there are some indications that the children's thinking was guided by one or more of these factors. Now let us look at the second area of study.

Buying from the rival store

The first extract is from Transcript A in Cappodocia Store. Storekeepers from Nicosia Store, Binnur, Funda and Göksel, decide to visit as customers and buy some items from Şefik in Cappodocia Store.

Extract 6.2.1

92	Funda		*Geliyor.*	(They are) coming
93	Binnur	(anxious to Şefik)	Hurry up!	
94	Şefik		*Bak! on bin, üç bin, dört bin.*	Look! Ten thousand, three thousand, four thousand.
95	Binnur	(to Sefik)	Wait! Shut up!	
96	Şefik	(To Binnur)	Don't tell me to shut up!	
		(To the visiting customers).	Look! You turn the car around!	
		(to Göksel)	Ten pounds.	
97	Göksel		I buy Kellogs corn flakes	
98	Şefik		Ehmm... ten pounds	
99	Funda	(to Şefik)	You got something. Give him his change!	
100	Şefik		Ten pounds.	
101	Binnur	(to Şefik)	Let's go to them.	
102	Funda		*Ha dur bende geleyim*	Wait for me!
			Hade gaç. Go away!	Go away!
103	Funda	(to other storekeepers)	We gonna come to you!	
104	Binnur	(repeating Funda's point)	We gonna come to you just get lost!	

Transcript A (Cappodocia Store): 92 -104 Funda, Şefik, Binnur, Göksel

Here the children set the terms and conditions of buying: who would buy, who would visit, when, how much they would be charged, how much change should be given etc. The storekeepers from Nicosia Store visit Cappodocia Store and Göksel buys corn-flakes for ten pounds, undeterred by the price.

This extract shows the children not yet negotiating the terms of the transaction, such as relating the prices they are charged as customers to the prices they charge in their own store.

The next extract is from Transcript A. The storekeepers from Cappodocia Store have phoned Nicosia Store to check if they may visit it.

Extract 6.2.2

192	Binnur		Knock. Knock!
193	Emine		Come in.
194	Şefik		Can we buy Tango?
195	Göksel		Yeah! How much?
196	Şefik	(someone laughs)	Ehm..
197	Göksel		We still haven't got any Tango.
			Oh!
		(He is told to carry on playing the game)	Yeah..Yeah..Yeah.
198	Emine		Five pounds.
199	Şefik	(astonished)	Five pounds for a Tango!
200	Göksel		It's a whole box.
201	Şefik		A whole box!
202	Binnur		What's this?
203	Şefik		Is there any fireworks?
204	Binnur		A fruit. I have this.

Extract 6.2.2 (continued)

205	Şefik	(to Binnur)	Buy this!
206	Binnur		What is it?
207	Şefik		Polo.
208	Binnur		No!
209	Şefik		Through (?) Polo.
210	Funda		How much is this?
211	Emine		Twenty p.
212	Funda	(to Şefik)	That's enough! You are not going to leave anything in their store!
213	Banu		Ice cream.
214	Şefik	(inspecting)	This is nice. This is nice.
215	Banu		One pound.
216	Binnur	(to Funda)	What are you doing?
217	Funda		You owe me.
218	Göksel	(to Şefik)	*Be!* Give me them! Hey!
219	Funda		You owe me!
220	Binnur		I get everything, there is hardly anything in their store.
221	Göksel	(to Binnur)	Let's go!
222	Binnur	(protesting about the prices on items)	Ten pounds, eleven pounds! What?
223	Göksel	(Supporting her)	Yes. That's what I have been saying!

Transcript A (Nicosia Store): 192-223 Şefik, Binnur, Funda, Göksel, Emine, Banu

This conversation supports points discussed earlier. As anticipated, the children performed the task of buying as if it were essentially a game, and with no idea about precisely what they were going to buy, concern for prices, or the need to specify quantities. It was not expected that they would think or make predictions in this first activity. They were trying to familiarise themselves with the basic rules of store roles and exchanging goods for money, rather than with buying as an activity based on their relating needs and their financial situation.

Both extracts from Transcript A should be seen in this light . The activities relating to buying – and indeed all the activities in the study – were to facilitate children's thinking. Situations such as the competition game were created with this in mind and it appears that these do to some extent facilitate their thinking.

During the visit Şefik is amazed by the price asked for a Tango (199), until assured by Göksel that this was for a whole box. Nicosia Store did not appear very organised in their pricing (211), although the price for Polos seems reasonable, indeed close to the actual cost of Polos in 1993.

The storekeepers in Cappodocia Store are fairly sure of the prices they would like for their goods, as we see by Banu's confusion when she discovers the wrong price labels on some items (222).

The visiting customers appear to be fairly satisfied with the prices demanded, and pay up happily. The lack of confrontation may also be due to the absence at this stage of competition or of the storekeepers' need to take their monetary situation into consideration.

This extract shows that the buyers gave little thought to processes of buying from another store, whereas the sellers were somewhat more organised about their pricing of goods. The earlier transcript, 6.1.2, shows their consistence when fixing their prices. To see changes in sellers' thinking, we need to turn to the next transcript, made seven months later.

In Transcript B, a buyer from Cappodocia Store (Şefik in role) is sent by his colleagues to buy some melons from Nicosia Store.

That the children are willing to play the game is clear from their reminders to each other (42). Binnur's instruction is accepted by Şefik but not by Göksel, who only speaks once, apparently coming out of role to point out a crisis (50). Şefik's response is to invite Göksel back into the game (52).

Extract 6.2.3

42	Binnur	(whispering to Funda)	Speak Turkish!	
43	Funda	(to Şefik)	*Ne isten?*	Would do you like?
44	Şefik		*Karpuz.*	
45	Funda		*Büyükler altı lira küçükler de üç lira!*	The big ones are six pounds and small ones are three.
			Istersen denersin.	You can try if you want.
46	Şefik		*Alırım.*	I'll buy.
47	Funda		*Büyük mü küçük mü?*	Big ones or small ones?
48	Şefik		*Büyük.*	A big one.
49	Funda		*Altı lira lütfen.*	Six pounds please.
50	Göksel		I have to give him four pounds change from ten pounds but there are no good coins.	
51	Funda	(tells Göksel off for not pretending)	You didn't even do it stupid! Do it!	
52	Şefik	(to Göksel, laughing)	Just pretend!	

Transcript B (Nicosia Store): 42-52 Binnur, Funda, Göksel, Şefik

---

The buyer from Cappodocia Store does not appear to be questioning the price being asked despite having a valid reason for doing so: comparing it to the price of the same item in his store (extract 6.1.2). Şefik appears either to have forgotten this or thought it unimportant. This extract is from the crucial moment in the competition when the storekeepers set out to make money for their stores in order to win. The storekeepers in Nicosia Store adjust their price of melons to seven pounds so they can make a profit (Transcript B, Cappodocia Store/82). Cappodocia's store-keepers understand the relationship between buying and selling price and making profit. The children did not use the word profit but their conversation indicates that they have some understanding of the concept. But the children's lack of action in crucial moments of the competition when shops were trying to raise money from their sales suggested otherwise. For instance the price asked for a melon (six pounds) in Nicosia Store was not challenged by the visiting customer from Cappodocia Store, even though it was at a critical stage in the competition. The visiting customer paying more meant more money coming out of their shop kitty, which could have lost them the competition.

The keepers of Cappodocia decided to raise their selling price to one pound above the price they paid in order to make a profit. The price does not appear to be evaluated in terms of its attractiveness to their own customers, although this is surely an important variable in competitive shopkeeping . But the children do show awareness of other variables in their thinking, and make subsequent decisions in the competition context (see the analysis under Cost, on page 62).

These extracts reveal certain differences in the way children respond to the process of buying from the rival store. While the examples from the initial transcript (6.1.1) show, as anticipated, the terms and conditions of the transaction processes, the extracts that followed in Transcript B appear to indicate some subtle differences in the way children perceive such transactions. While the storekeepers in Cappodocia Store question the prices charged for items, the other group did not ask such questions. Nor did they offer their buyers any alternative explanations for why their own prices were too high. There was also little discussion between themselves – as buyers – about the prices charged by the other store, so we have no insight into their strategies. We do know, however, that the Cappodocia storekeepers thought about the price charged by Nicosia and adjusted their own selling prices in order to make money.

These findings again challenge the theories that children's economic understanding of profit develops in prescribed stages, as put forward by Strauss (1952), Furth (1978) and Danziger (1958). All these argued that children follow similar stages in their development and suggest median ages for children's understanding of profit: Strauss 9.9, Furth 10.7, and Danziger as early as 8.0. Although these studies give different chronological ages for the understanding of profit they are in agreement on the specific age range at which it occurs. Jahoda (1979), who adopted a slightly different approach, setting up interactive role-playing shop contexts to evaluate children's understanding of profit, concluded that children reached this stage at age ten.

The children from Cappodocia Store who showed some understanding of profit fit within the age range put forward by Furth and others (three of the children were aged between 9.3 and 9.10). This does not tell us much, as the range outlined by Danziger and others is quite wide and it is likely that most children will show some understanding of profit within this wide spectrum. But the theorists of stages do not tell us, for example, why despite falling within the age range 9.4-9.11, the storekeepers in Nicosia Store do *not* appear to have any understanding of profit. It is also apparent that the children's understanding of various conceptual areas differs widely, supporting the view that children learn through a variety of experiences.

I argue that children's conceptual development is not a matter of linear progression through stages, but is shaped in the context of diverse experiences. Children's learning in a particular conceptual area takes place through various complex and interrelated experiences. It is inaccurate to call these levels, because this suggests a hierarchical and sequential structure in the way children acquire understanding. Children's perceptions and interpretations achieved through particular learning experiences are acquired at various times and with varying intensity. The process depends on the interactive activity undertaken, the language of interaction, the children's cultural experiences (individual and social) and on their age. We saw how some children in Nicosia Store who showed scant understanding of profit showed understanding in other conceptual areas.

Children were asked to negotiate prices for items in their shops as well in the other shop they visited as customers, but prices were not always reduced in response. This made it difficult to establish how the children thought about these variables. Did storekeepers reduce prices to make money so they could win the competition? The evidence indicates that children did so in some circumstances but not others. Why then did the children fail to discuss among themselves the prices they as rival buyers should charge? This failure may tell us something about the effects of rivalry on children's thinking and may even explain some of the ways in which children think and behave in different contexts.

The findings in this section on profit appear to support those in the first section about cost: learning contexts and activities affect children's conceptual development. Development is also influenced by the cultural experiences each child brings to the learning context. Vygotsky (1978) maintained that children's cultural development occurred at both societal and individual levels. He believed that the child develops through actively participating in interactions with peers and adults as well as constructing meaning for himself/herself. And these experiences are acquired, negotiated and transmitted through appropriate tools of communication – that is through language. In this study the development in children's thinking about the prices charged by the wholesaler are embedded in and negotiated through the children's discussions in Turkish and English. These are explored in the context of Vygotsky's ideas of cultural development. Bilingual children's conceptual development must be evaluated in the bilingual context in which it takes place. This is discussed further in the next section.

Summary on the concept of buying

Exploring bilingual children's development in a bilingual context is important for two reasons. Firstly, their individual and social development takes place in the context of two languages, so ignoring one part of their interaction would result in the evaluating just one dimension of their development and the findings would be seriously inadequate. Secondly, bilingual children use both their languages. Knowledge acquired through experience is often evaluated through their own cross-channel communication.[1] This suggests a complex interactive relationship between the two languages, in which the child is constantly processing and evaluating new information by drawing upon the resources available in one or both languages. Bilingual learning must be perceived in the context of such a relationship.

This analysis supports findings related to the other conceptual areas discussed earlier. Children's ideas about buying from the wholesaler were analysed in relation to several variables and we

saw that children did not think about prices or show much awareness of the variables during the initial activities. In later extracts
they appear to be reflecting on their previous actions, re-evaluat-
ing their earlier conclusions. There was evidence that children
were considering more than one variable in relation to buying
from the wholesaler. Studies of bilingual children's thinking supports the view that bilinguals perform more flexibly than their
monolingual peers in their fluency, originality and elaboration in
thinking (Baker, 1988; Ricciardelli, 1992). Cummins (1977)
found bilinguals to be more fluent and flexible than monolinguals.
The ability of the children running Cappodocia Store to analyse
the variables affecting price indicates such flexibility.

Flexibility has been investigated by a number of researchers who
concentrate on processes rather than products of thinking
(Kardash *et al.*, 1988; Bialystok, 1991). These children's prompt
responses to researcher-initiated conversation supports their findings. Often when I suggested a new idea, they were very quick to
act on it (see extract 6.1.3 in the appendix).

Children's bilingualism has also been studied for communicative
sensitivity, that is, the ability to organise their linguistic choices
appropriately: when to speak which language. Baker (1996) describes communicative sensitivity as

> The need constantly to monitor what is the appropriate language
> in which to respond or when initiating a conversation. (p136)

Ben Zeev's comparative study of monolingual and bilingual children (1977) found bilinguals to be more responsive to hints and
clues in the experimental situation. The children in my study appear to prefer Turkish when playing the game and speak to the
researcher in Turkish also, as they regard his role as part of the
game. Initially the children responded to the researcher in Turkish,
but switched to English to talk among themselves, but later
examples show them speaking Turkish even when he was not
participating in the game.

In the second section, a similar picture emerged. The children
determined the terms of interaction for the game they were to
play. The conditions changed: they now appeared to see this as
their game, which *they* would decide how to play. Francis (1998)
looked at interactive group processes as a source of power for each
gender group, arguing that gender discourses impacted on pupils'

construction of power. The children's determination about their roles shown in my study appears to support Francis' findings about children's construction of power in relation to gender but here they were operating from their perception of themselves in a specific role dealing with particular tasks. Those who had power used it to position themselves as organisers of others[2] – what Francis calls 'active in positioning' (1998, p7). Foucault (1980) argued that personality is fixed and that people are positioned and position others through discourse and – as Francis maintains – that power is embedded in the discourse of socially and culturally produced patterns of language (cited in Francis 1998, p7).

It was predominantly girls who took the lead in initiating the discussions in my study and the boys who followed. Together they acted as a coherent and efficient group. They shared responsibilities and each tried to do their share. Their insistence on speaking Turkish may indicate that they wished to stick to the rules of the game.

The interactions may have been influenced by the terms determined for them. They interacted with the wholesaler – the researcher in role – in the first section, but had much greater autonomy in Section Two. They were in charge and they knew the rules of the game. And they knew when the person pretending to be a customer was really a rival from the other store.

The examples generated in the course of this study did not provide sufficient data to analyse all the possible variables. But subtle differences could be observed in the way children in Cappodocia Store thought and how they interpreted the prices charged by the rival store to determine the prices for their customers. By the end of these activities the children began to show, in their thinking and actions, that they understood that the activity of buying is influenced by several factors.

It is difficult to identify clear examples of children's thinking regarding their understanding of each factor. Their thinking does not manifest itself in clear and orderly messages but more often in disjointed and disconnected comments.

I also tried to relate specific aspects of children's thinking to other experiences from home or school but could only observe one child at home on one occasion (see Transcript A, extract 4.1.3 in the appendix). The findings in this section do, however, highlight the importance of the organisation of interactive activities. Margaret Donaldson (1978) has shown that children are able to cope with tasks much earlier than predicted if these are presented clearly and in a way that makes sense to them. In this study, the children's understanding of profit appeared to develop through the informal role-playing activities, which were related to their experiences of real shop transactions. Consequently, their understanding of profit was due to the activities organised and also the cultural and social experiences the children brought into learning situations. Such factors were not sufficient, however, to help develop the Nicosia Store children's understanding of profit, but did so for those in Cappodocia.

Children's cultural and social experiences are extensive and diverse and they affect each child differently. This applies also to organised activities, as each one is perceived and interpreted differently by every child. The picture is complex.

To conclude: the examples used did not always yield enough information to analyse the variables surrounding the process of buying fully. However, the children's discussions did provide sufficient data to conclude that the children, especially in the later activities, were showing growing awareness of the existence of the many variables. We saw bilingual children using reflective and communicative skills, and some of them did show understanding of profit. Using their two languages interchangably contributed to such understanding as concepts and ideas flowed freely between the two language mediums.

Notes

1 For example, the child discovers the meaning for a new word in Turkish, *karpuz*, by seeking appropriate attachments for equivalent names for objects in English. Through such a mechanism the child discovers that the English word *melon* has the same attachment hence the 'large oval shaped fruit with thick green skin' has two name tags attached.

2 The relationship between boys and girls as described by Francis was based on power. However in the same study, the girls who always had the authority in decision making process often chose to 'exercise' their authority in view of collective gains for the *whole* group.

7

Children's understanding
of work

The final area explored in my study is the ideas children have about work. I looked at children's interpretations of it under three headings:

- work as the sharing of collective responsibilities – children's thoughts as shown through their organisation of routine tasks

- work as the division of labour: children's perceptions of organising the division of responsibilities in running their company

- work as a task undertaken in exchange for money: children's ideas on the relationship between work done and money earned.

1 Work as sharing of collective responsibilities

Three transcripts were made in this section and I use examples from the first (7.1.1) and the last (7.1.3) extracts. The first is from Transcript B in the Nicosia Store where the storekeepers are making price and name labels for their store.

This extract shows children organising the tasks at hand. They appear to be working in harmony and are busily sharing the responsibility for cutting out and labelling items, making extra picture labels in addition to the ones supplied by the researcher. They respond positively to requests from each other about individual

---

Extract 7.1.1

6	Funda	(to Binnur)	Let's cut this.	
			Göksel! Go and get a scissors.	
		(to Göksel)		
7	Binnur	(to Göksel)	Get two if there is two.	
8	Funda		What shall I do?	
9	Binnur		Just cut those in half.	
10	Funda		They can use them as tasters like they want to taste them.	
11	Göksel	(to Binnur)	Cut this half and colour in half of it!	
		calling for customers	*Karpuz var!*	Melons!
12	Binnur	(to Göksel)	Put the testers here. Let's cut this one!	
13	Göksel		We would sell them for two pounds. I cut this.	

Transcript B (Nicosia Store): 6-13 Göksel, Funda, Binnur,

---

tasks, for example Göksel's response to requests by Binnur and Funda (6/7). The storekeepers appear to be asking each other's advice on the tasks to be done. Göksel's sudden switch to Turkish supports the observation that children associate the use of Turkish with the role-play (11).

The last extract is from Transcript D, where the children are producing a bilingual newspaper with different columns. The 'editors' discuss what they should include in their paper.

Banu's proposition (109) indicates her willingness to listen to other ideas on the subject and contributes positively to the discussion. Generally the children listen to each other and put across their opinions. We see them thinking about how newspapers are compiled, as they leaf through the bilingual Turkish/English newspapers supplied. Banu's suggestion is inspired by a tabloid news-

Extract 7.1.3

106	Şefik	*Bir.. Bir...*One One	One ...One
107	Emine	She did do that!	
108	Funda	She did!	
109	Banu	What else shall we do?	
110	Birsen	We could put this an advertisement page.	
111	Banu	No! we could do that at the back.	
112	Şefik	At the back you could do sports.	
113	Emine	No! not right at the back.	
114	Banu	I know what we can do. Just small pieces of writing about something and then we will say continue on	
		sahifa.	Page.
115	Şefik	Like that in the *Sun* in it!	

Transcript D: 106-115 Banu, Birsen, Şefik

paper (114), and Şefik's proposal is accepted with some modifications (112). The children reach agreement about some of the columns for their paper, and respond favourably to each other's suggestions.

The two examples show that the children were aware of what was required of them and worked collaboratively to carry them out.

No child used the word 'work' but their use of expressions such as 'let's do...', in both languages, suggests an awareness that tasks must be done collectively.

The children generally appeared willing to role-play the stores games and the newspaper scenario. The use of Turkish during discussions in the researcher's absence supports this, and can be related to bilingual children's communicative sensitivity (see page 92, chapter 6). In one extract from this section, children talk about the tasks at hand and also make up stories about their 'other' lives, referring to their homes, and to missing their families (see extract 7.1.2 in the appendix).

The examples from the transcripts show that the interaction between the children increases as role plays progress. In the first two examples (extracts 7.1.1 and 7.1.2) certain children take the lead and urge others to do various tasks, but do not hesitate to ask each other for guidance. In the third extract (7.1.3, Transcript D), Şefik's involvement is particularly noticeable as he participates fully in the discussions, offering his views on sections of the newspaper (112/115). The children here appear much more confident about their tasks. This may be a reflection of their areas of interest and community links.[1] One of the children's parents owned a restaurant, and they knew the names of most Turkish stores in their local neighbourhood. Through the sequence of extracts we see increasing dynamism in the children's interactions.

Furth (1978) and Burris (1983), who both argue that experience is less significant than development stages in children's understanding economic concepts, have been challenged. Holroyd (1990, p109) asserts that

> There is no need to wait for readiness on the part of the children before introducing concepts to them. If they are presented in ways which make sense in the context of children's experience they will understand them.

This study confirms Holroyd's view: we can see by their level of verbal interaction that the children's confidence in the tasks is related to their experience. Şefik's involvement and interest reflects his interests outside school, in Turkish singers and football teams. Hutchings, too, emphasised the importance of relevant experiences as crucial in children's development of conceptual ideas (1990, p147).

2 Work as a division of responsibilities in a workplace

A total of three extracts have been recorded in this section and the first and the last extracts are set out here. The first example from Transcript C shows the children setting up a trucking company. They are discussing their individual responsibilities for the related tasks:

Extract 7.2.1

5	Banu		Alright I start.. I don't know what to say.
6	Binnur	(to Şefik)	You said you were the boss, you start.
7	Banu		I think we should start who wants to do what.
8	Şefik	(interrupting)	Shut up! Shut up!
9	Funda	(to Şefik)	You don't know what you are doing are you? What are you doing?
10	Göksel		Who wants to go to Cyprus?
11	Şefik		That's where I come from! I am going there.
12	Göksel		I am going there as well!
		(to Banu)	Who is staying with you?
13	Banu		We are all going to decide who and what we are.
14	Sefik		I am the boss!
15	Banu	(to Şefik)	We don't have much time OK!
16	Binnur		How many trucks are we gonna have?
17	Şefik		I wanna have..
18	Banu		Who will do... writing?
19	Göksel		Not me!
20	Banu		I don't want to write them.
21	Binnur		Alright! I will do it.

Transcript C : 5-21 Banu, Şefik, Göksel, Binnur, Funda

Banu starts the discussion by defining what the group should be considering (7). Şefik and Göksel want to simply do their own thing, and nominate themselves a visit to Cyprus (11/12). Having reached this decision, the boys decide to impose it on the others (12). The girls remind them that matters need to be discussed and agreed collectively. Note Banu's use of the word 'we' (13). _efik resists but Banu tells him to concentrate on the task (15). The boys then begin to respond positively. In this early discussion about who should do what, the girls appear to be more in tune with the requirements and they successfully get across to the boys the need for collective discussion.

In the third extract, also from Transcript C, the girls are discussing the finer points of taking things to and from Cyprus.

Extract 7.2.3

51	Binnur	If those (two) are driving who is going to collect the things we bring them?
52	Banu	Who is going to be our driver?
53	Funda	We will take turns.
54	Binnur	They are the drivers and they will take things to London remember!
55	Banu	Who will take things from London to Cyprus?
56	Binnur	Maybe Tözün will say you can't have it!
57	Banu	They [Sefik and Göksel] are gone and we have somebody else coming.
58	Binnur	Yeah! But they are in Cyprus and we are in London and we need the drivers because if somebody asks us to take something there they are not gonna come back again!

Transcript C: 51-58 Banu, Binnur, Funda

Binnur points out that extra help will be needed to collect, load and unload the melons once they have been delivered by Göksel and Şefik (51). Banu interprets the query differently (52). Binnur's query appears to be relating to bringing items from

Cyprus back to London. There seems to be an assumption by Binnur that the two drivers (Şefik and Göksel) are only taking goods from London to Cyprus. Binnur's final suggestion indicates that she would like their store to have extra drivers in case work comes their way while their drivers are in Cyprus (58), and she assumes that they might not come back. The children are beginning to think about the nature of the tasks in some detail, and taking them seriously.

These extracts indicate how the children worked as a coherent group to plan and review their allocated responsibilities, particularly the girls. We see progression in the development of children's thinking in the course of the session.

The first extract (7.2.1) sets the tone and direction of discussion. The gendered nature of the discussion is of note. The boys try to set the terms of negotiation by announcing what they want to do (7.2.1/11-12), whereas the girls relate scenario to issues of collective decision making about various tasks to good effect. The children then work coherently, and agree on individual responsibilities. Although the two extracts do not provide a full picture of all the decisions agreed by the children,[2] we get a clear sense of collaboration within the team.

The extracts can be analysed in terms of 'gender discourse' – the term Davies and Banks (1992) apply to describe all discourses concerning gender. Francis (1998) divided these into two separate groups: 'inequity discourses' which include 'all those (discourses) that present the genders as unequal and discriminate unfairly according to gender', and 'equity discourses' which include 'all those who oppose gender discrimination' (1998, p 140). Francis breaks these down further into categories, which are useful here.[3]

Boys made statements in extract 7.2.1 which Francis would describe as 'discourses of innate inequality' which, she argues, is often produced via children's narrative of 'male superiority and female inferiority' (1998:144). No narratives of 'female superiority' were found in my transcripts. The girls' responses can rather be categorised as 'genders should have equal opportunity', which Francis argues is based on children's perceptions about fairness (1998: 143). Francis, like Lloyd and Duveen (1992) and Damon (1977), found that the values of fairness begin to outweigh children's identification of sex roles from the age of seven. Contrary to findings by Francis and others, 'fairness' was evident in the girls' perception of the boys' behaviour towards themselves. My findings also run counter to Francis' finding that children failed to 'challenge' the dominant constructed gender dichotomy (1998:147). Here the girls not only put forward their views on fairness but also challenged boys' idea about dominance (7.2.1/Utterance 13).

The second and third extracts show the children's sense of organisation becoming clearer. Having agreed on the terms of negotiation, they start discussing individual responsibilities when, in extract 7.2.1, Göksel and Şefik declare that they will go to Cyprus. The girls initially oppose this but then think again and agree that they should be the drivers for the company. Thus a potential power conflict between the sexes is avoided.

The children understand how to run their company, and the third extract in particular supports this. Their careful analysis of the details of the transporting arrangement (7.2.3) and their discussion and clarification of the problems and the possibilities for remedying them give the impression of a well co-ordinated and efficient team who understand what the task involves.

3 Work done in exchange for money – 'paid work'

Only two examples of children's perceptions relating to work done in exchange for money reflect variations in the children's thinking from those analysed earlier. Both are given here.

The first extract is from Transcript C, where I visit the storekeepers and inquire about how their truck company is progressing.

Extract 7.3.1

107	Researcher	*Nasıl gidiyor?*	How is it going?
108	Binnur	*Para gelmiyor biz de iş yapmıyoruz.*	There is no money coming in so we are not doing any work.
109	Researcher	*Müşterileriniz yok mu yani?*	You mean you have no customers?
110	Şefik	*Yok.!*	None!

Extract 7.3.1 (continued)

111	Researcher	*Kim gidiyor Kıbrısa?*	Who is going to Cyprus?
		Başka ne probleminiz var?	What other problems do you have?
112	Binnur	*Müsteri gelmiyor!*	There is no customers coming!
113	Researcher	*Kumpanyanızı kurdunuz mu?*	Did you set up your company?
114	Banu	*Evet !*	Yes!
115	Researcher	*Kaç tane TIR aldınız?*	How many trucks did you buy?
116	Banu	*Üç!*	Three!
117	Researcher	*Parayı nerden buldunuz?*	Where did you get the money from?
118	Binnur	*Babamızdan aldık.*	We got it from our dads.
119	Şefik	Robbed a bank!	
120	Binnur	*Çok çalışmalıyız çünkü borç ödeyeceğiz!*	We must work really hard because we are going to pay our debts.
121	Researcher	*Ofiste kim kalacak?*	Who will stay in the office?
122	Banu/Binnur/Funda	*Biz!*	Us!
123	Researcher	*TIR' ları burdan Kıbrısa kim sürecek?*	Who will drive the trucks to Cyprus?
124	Binnur	*Ben sürerim o zaman!*	I will drive in that case!

Transcript C: 107-124 Banu, Sefik, Funda, Researcher

Binnur's response to me (108) shows her awareness of the relationship between *para* (money) and doing 'business' but she is the only child who uses the word *para* in her conversation. They realise that money is needed to set up a business, as I elicit by my questioning (117-118). Şefik's response (119) was meant as a joke, although it also indicates his understanding of banks as the places where money is kept. Although the responses were generally brief and unelaborated, there appears to be general understanding of the relationship between work and money. Binnur is the only child who elaborated on the topic without any direct prompting (120).

Binnur also shows her understanding of the relationship between work and paying off debts (120), using the Turkish word for work, *çalışmak*, when she communicates her ideas.

In the second extract from Transcript D, children discuss various sections to be included in their newspaper. They have been given sample Turkish and English newspapers to help them with their ideas.

Extract 7.3.2

10	Şefik	Who can write in Turkish?	
11	Funda	I can!	
12	Şefik	I can't!	
13	Funda	Before that *makina yapardık* with my dad's thing.	(literally) making machine
14	Şefik (trying to read something from the Turkish newspaper)	Advertised!	
15	Banu (Looking at one of the adverts in the Turkish paper)	This man used to come to my dad's restaurant and sing there	

Transcript D: 10-15 Şefik, Banu, Funda

Funda is referring (13) to a family printing store where she has seen printing being done for customers. Her comment in Turkish is about her father's printing with his machine. Similarly, Banu refers to a person singing in her father's restaurant (15).

Both the girls have experience of money being paid for work. Banu may have observed the singer being paid or the customers paying their bills in return for their meal. Funda had noted transactions where customers paid for the printing services provided by her father. Although there is no direct evidence, Funda and Banu may well have observed their fathers paying for goods too.

The examples given by the children reflect their experiences within their family businesses and shows that some of them were aware of the links between work and money, but we cannot make generalisations about all children's understanding.

Both extracts show some understanding of the relationship between earning money and doing work and between 'doing business' (selling items) and 'earning money'. What is unclear is whether the children regarded the act of selling as work.[4] Although they do make reference to work in extract 7.3.2 it is not clear whether they understand the relationship. However, other reflections about their first hand experience of family workplaces shows that some children have taken note of transactions where money was used to pay for the services provided by, for example, wholesalers, workers and customers. Hutchings (1990) describes this as what children call 'job work', to describe all forms of paid work: employment and self-employment. She observes that children often have experience of paid work 'before they leave primary school, either working within the family or being employed by neighbours'. Children who have directly experienced transactions are likely to have developed some understanding of the relationship between money and work (1990:148).

Conclusions on the concept of work

Unlike studies such as those of Hutchings, 1990 and Ross, 1990, my study was not designed to find direct references to work. However, the references to children's home working environments suggest that children were aware of the process involved in buying and selling and had some ideas about what different people *did* as work. They knew that people worked in restaurants, bought items from a printer shop, and that the printer bought card from wholesaler, all of which suggests that the children understood the relationship between people working and the kinds of 'job work' described by Hutchings (1990).

The store organisational context was analysed to evaluate children's skill at sharing routine tasks. The children were well organised and shared tasks collectively. The boys wanted to do their own thing but were made to listen and became included in the decision making processes. Thus we see those who are often identified as treated unfairly – girls – challenging the boys and also organising an inclusive strategy for the benefit of the whole group.

In the next set of extracts similar patterns emerged. Organisational points initiated by the girls determined the decisions taken by the whole group. Decisions were taken on the principle of what was best for the whole group rather than the interests of individual children, in this case the boys as we saw when the girls finally accepted that Şefik and Göksel's should take the role of drivers (extract 7.2.1).

The examples suggest that the children had already thought about areas of responsibility by organising themselves before I questioned them. This confirms findings that children interpret work as varied, broad and multi-dimensional rather than cognitive and evolving in clearly defined stages. My study shows that children's development of the concept of work depends on a variety of factors, among them their cultural experiences.

In the next chapter I explore how children's bilingual thinking can positively contribute to their understanding of related concepts, providing a selection of strategies and practical examples for teachers.

Notes

1 Children were constantly talking about their favourite Turkish singers and football teams.

2 For example we are not sure of the responsibilities agreed for Banu and Binnur.

3 Many examples in Francis' study reflected children's responses to questions by the researcher. For example Francis indicates that children frequently drew upon what she calls 'genders should have equal opportunities' discourses. When asked whether an employer would gender differentiate in job allocation, children responded by saying 'all the jobs should be for men, 'cos who's gonna look after the children?' Francis used this example to show that children, despite making statements on 'genders should illustrate have equal opportunities' discourses, do anything to support their views. This is due to the general nature of questioning and the generality of the discussions, which are quite unlike the present study.

4 Except Binnur who appears to demonstrate her understanding by using the word *çalışmak*, *(work)* in Turkish.

8

Implications for classroom practice

This chapter describes the implications of some of my findings for classroom practice. How can class teachers create opportunities to exploit the special abilities of bilingual pupils?

Getting to know our pupils

The first step is to get to know our pupils. Who are they? What kind of experiences are they exposed to at home and in their communities? In what situations do they use their first languages? To answer such questions a number of informal activities and discussions need to be initiated to give children opportunities to talk about themselves and their home experiences. Children need to feel confident about sharing this information with their teachers and peers without fear of being ridiculed by the rest of the class.

Diagnostic information

Teachers are already required to produce substantive records of children's work for assessment purposes. These include relevant information about children's home backgrounds and the languages spoken at home. There are also records of tests, classroom activities and children's attainment in core national curriculum subjects. In English particularly, there is evidence of children's performance in three key areas, Speaking and Listening, Reading, and Writing. In my recent teaching experience as a class teacher and also in my classroom observations it was evident that the first of these, speaking and listening, remains the least explored in the classrooms. But as the previous chapter has revealed, this area offers teachers particularly valuable opportunities for developing the abilities of bilingual learners.

There are ample opportunities for teachers to find out about children's home and community experiences. As well as the weekend tasks for their diaries, other written assignments, whether factual or imaginative, offer opportunities for teachers to explore each child's unique world. Asking children to write an account of an incident they have witnessed on the way to school or to produce a recipe for a local delicacy provides valuable information for the teacher.

This applies equally to reading. Asking children to read something of their own choice gives teachers an idea of their interests, relevant experiences, likes and dislikes as well as their thinking on particular texts. While these activities doubtless develop relevant skills in children, they are not sufficient in themselves to help bilingual children reach their full potential. Every activity needs to be set up with specific tasks for developing speaking and listening skills as well as reading and writing to support the learning outcomes for the teacher. An example, opposite, from a Literacy lesson plan for a year four class illustrates how it can be done.

Here the particular tasks for reading, writing, speaking and listening are drawn up in relation to the learning outcomes set for the lesson. Sometimes there are opportunities for class teachers to work and deliver the lesson jointly with specialist language teachers on the EMA team. The planning for speaking and listening can be fine tuned – the teachers discuss each stage of the delivery of the lesson together, so ensuring maximum benefit for the bilingual learners.

Any activity should require children to articulate their ideas and thinking, so helping them sound out their ideas, evaluate their thinking in view of their peers' responses and, most importantly, giving teachers information about children's thinking. One of the ways this can be done is through creating classroom situations for facilitating purposeful talk, such as reflecting particular cultural experiences that the children bring into the classroom. For example

Lesson aim	Book	Lesson Structure	Tasks	Materials
To develop the use of expressive language to create moods in text level work	*The Taniwha of Grafton Gully*	**Whole class teaching** Book presented to whole class with setting and descriptive words discussed. Chart prepared to use descriptions, e.g. monster's character and setting to be filled in jointly with whole class. **Group activity** (pairs) Children are given a chart with a list of descriptions to be sorted into relevant spaces in the chart **Plenary** pairs to give their descriptions of the monster while the other pupil draws it on the board	• **Reading** children to read and sort relevant descriptive words into a chart. Also reading words in Maori language • **Writing** Using a writing frame to construct sentences about the monster and setting and using adjectives and other expressive words in shared writing, followed by focused group work • **Speaking and listening:** Discuss with your partner which descriptions to use for relevant spaces on the chart Also discuss which words in your home language support Maori words • **Plenary** Decide who will do what, who will draw the descriptions, who will do the report back	• Charts with key descriptive, expressive words Enlarged text with a picture of the monster Also similar words in Maori and some words from the languages spoken in the class • Pictures of people, showing expression, moods, action to support key vocabulary used Source: *Naldic Literacy Papers* (1998)

asking a pupil to speak in more detail about the weekend experience she described in her writing would also reveal something of her community involvement. Many bilingual children attend supplementary schools during the weekend and these community activities can be used by the teacher for purposeful learning, as shown later in this chapter.

Experiences embedded within home and community can be described in English, but the full impact is best made through the first language. We see this in a child's description of the festival of *Eid*, or *Bayram* as it is called in Turkish. The child's interpretation of the ritual of kissing the hand of her grandparents to symbolise respect can only have full impact when it is articulated in Turkish. And it allows her to explore and organise her own thinking before transferring the account into English. The teacher's role is to enable this to happen naturally, by making provision for oral accounts in both languages.

We know that children are reluctant for various reasons to participate in activities where they are asked to use their home languages. The reasons can be traced back to historical developments relating to bilingualism in the UK, details of which I will not go into here. However it is fair to say that the structure of the English national curriculum allows little flexibility for using anything but English in the classroom and it is left to the individual initiative of teachers. Schools are required to adhere to the national standards in English and the performance of school is measured accordingly. In one extreme case I witnessed a teacher openly reprimanding children for speaking their own languages in the classroom as they were discussing the task set for them. Children sense whether or not their home language is welcome in the classrooms.

The other restriction relates to peer group influence. Children do not want to be different and always strive to be like the rest of the group. So they may be reluctant to use their home language in the classroom. It needs to be facilitated through planned activities that boost children's confidence about expressing their own experiences in their first language.

Facilitating natural talk in the classroom

Before talking about planning more activities for the use of first languages, teachers should create situations for natural, random use of them so as to boost children's confidence about using their own languages, for example:

■ **An integrated topic on countries of the world, languages, people and customs**
Such topics provide starting points for discussions on how people live and the languages spoken in each country. They help children identify with that country and language. Children are then used as 'experts' on their country of origin, by being asked to provide meanings to certain words, names of food and so on. This is a real boost to their confidence. I have seen from experience that children absolutely love this role of expert.

■ **Ask children to bring in a recipe from their country of origin**
Children exhibit great pride and enjoyment when asked to teach the class how to make a traditional dish from their country of origin. Parents could also be involved in this. Seeing their parents in the classroom gives children great confidence about their own languages. Such activities convey very positive messages about the use of other languages and customs in the classroom.

■ **Hold general class discussions about 'people around us'**
This can take place at circle time or during a plenary at the end of a lesson. Such discussions provide opportunities for the teacher to link the general topic on countries to a more specific one on people we see around us. Usually pictures and other visual resources help to dispel stereotypes and clarify any myths or misunderstanding by the children, for example about clothing or certain visible characteristics displayed by the people. Regular discussions of this nature provide a firm basis for challenging prejudices such as racism and sexism and help promote linguistic diversity as an asset in the classroom.

■ **Create frequent opportunities for children to translate their work from the home language to English**
These could take the form of written work done at supplementary school or related to a classroom task, for example a description of a religious event or cultural ceremony. Or it might be about a recent visit to their country of origin and a description of a market place or national festival. This gives

children the chance to articulate their ideas in their first language and then transfer them into English. Having two children standing side by side and reading the two language versions of the same work written by one of them gives the right message to the class about the equal status of both languages. This is a particularly useful activity for asylum seekers or those who may be new to English.

Similar approaches can be used in reading – a child reads a story in one language while the other translates it simultaneously into English. Thus all the children are given insight into stories of other cultures and the status of the home language is raised.

Warm up activities give class teachers valuable information about the languages used at home and the contexts in which they are used. For example, wedding parties are regular cultural events in which children take part and which they might like to describe. And we have seen how the economic activities of the Turkish/ Kurdish communities can be used in the classroom. Teachers should find other community-specific activities that reflect their pupils' experiences. Once teachers are informed about activities of this kind, they can organise more structured activities in the classroom. Below are some examples.

■ **Ask your partner**
This can be the first step towards developing children's speaking and listening skills. It can be used in any part of the lesson to support teacher's planned discussion and introduction to the lesson. For example during the Literacy Hour, before introducing the book *The Three Billy Goats Gruff*, the teacher may decide to sound out what children already know about animals by asking them if they have ever been on a farm and which animals they have seen.

> I would like you to turn to your partner and ask them if they have been to a farm and which animals they have seen.

The children have to report back what their partner said. This short activity not only provides a good framework for introducing the story but also encourages purposeful talk and develops children's listening skills. Such activities are particularly useful for younger children and, while developing their oral skills, they are also good preparation for working in larger groups. The next activity is an example of larger group work (4-6 children) and encourages collaboration and teamwork.

Collaborative group activities

There is a long and distinguished history of collaborative learning, where emerging bilinguals are placed in groups where there are English monolinguals and, ideally, bilingual children whose English is more advanced. If the task is interesting, this structure encourages those new to English to contribute. The main purpose of group activities is to help children learn to function as a group and learn from one another. So it is important to think carefully about how to organise these groups. Personality and gender balances should be considered as well as the range of abilities. It is important to place new arrivals and refugees in pairs, and follow the discussion by group work where they have access to good models of spoken English. The following activities are planned to facilitate group interaction and debate and to address relevant learning outcomes. The first example is of paired work to prepare children for larger group activities. Paired activities can also help prepare children for the main part of the lesson.

Subject topic: Vehicles and Pollution
Year 5 Class

Learning outcomes: Children will be able to

- list three things they would like to do to prevent pollution
- discuss how they will go about doing it
- report back to the whole class

After introducing the activity it is important to brainstorm the idea. There are two reasons for this: it reinforces what children already know on the topic and helps teachers plan and extend children's learning further. Putting up ideas on a board helps remind the pupils about the point of the discussion and provides vocabulary. In order to cater for the varying abilities in the classrooms a mixture of open ended and closed questions such as How..? Why..? Where..? need to be asked, to help the pupils focus on the topic. A fairly straightforward question like 'Can a car run on water?' or 'What do cars need to move?' usually gets everybody's attention before more open ended questions are asked, for example 'What do you think happens to our atmosphere as carbon monoxide is given out by the exhaust fumes?'

When children are put into groups their tasks need to be clearly explained. Set them out on the board for clarity.

Decide who will write down the points, who will report back to the class and who will be the timekeeper.

During the activities the teacher moves around the groups to keep the children on task. During the initial sessions not much work is likely to be done and children may not seem to be functioning as a group. This is to be expected, especially if children have had little practice working in groups. The teacher's role is to guide pupils towards the task, resolve any tensions between them and guide them in the right direction in their discussion by asking relevant questions. Try to deal with any conflict of personalities that may emerge during the group activities and try to prevent one or two people from dominating. The object is to give all the children opportunities to speak and express their views. Inevitably, some children will be silent because they are shy or feel dominated by the others but everything should be done to enable all members of the group to contribute, in their home language or English. Changing the groups or talking to the child about their problems or otherwise persevering usually produces results. Do not expect too much.

Before the plenary make sure that each group is agreed about what they have discussed and the spokesperson knows exactly what he/she is reporting back. Children need to be aware of the importance of listening to each other when groups report back and learn to respect each other's views. Ensure that if children want to add information they are given opportunities to do so and that all the pupils understand all that has been said.

After the report back the teacher summarises the main points of discussion and highlights possible points for future debate. Provided that the children observe the routines planned by the teacher, each session should become progressively more manageable – and less noisy. My own experience showed me that by the third or fourth session children begin responding to the demands of the task with enthusiasm. Age, abilities and relevant discussion experiences play a part but it is crucial to go over the rules of the activity very carefully before each session and make sure that all the children understand them thoroughly.

Once such activities have become part of the class routine, the children will become more confident about using their home languages. This will enable the teacher to plan more structured group activities so that each is cognitively and linguistically more demanding. The examples below could be the first and the last in a series of planned activities. The key point to consider in all of them is that children are given focus ideas, usually conflict situations, to explore and resolve and then are left to their own devices to use their languages naturally and interchangeably in order to find collective solutions. The topics are chosen from culturally relevant areas reflecting children's experiences.

Example 1
Role-play scenario: An Accident and Emergency department in a London hospital.

Introduction: before explaining the task the teacher needs to have a general discussion and a brainstorming session in which children are asked about their experience of hospitals. The point is to make sure that children have an idea about how AE departments looks and some of the procedures involved.

Setting the context: children are given a briefing for the activity. The teacher explains that this is a scene from a London hospital where people from different backgrounds receive treatment. The children will be asked to perform a scene from a casualty department where a man who has just had an accident is brought in. The emergency team will need to attend to him but there is problem.

Point to consider: despite his injuries the person can talk – but he can't speak English. The medical team needs to attend to him urgently to find out the extent of his injuries. How are they going to deal with this?

The children are put into groups of eight to discuss their roles. The children need to be aware that the person they choose to be the 'patient' must speak another language in addition to English.

This is particularly important in instilling a sense of responsibility in the children and it is amazing how much they rise to this. Nonetheless careful consideration needs to be given to the formation of the groups. It is also expected that some children will have more ideas than others. So the groups need sufficient time to organise themselves, discuss how they will go about performing and then give the actual performance. It is important to have the groups watch each other perform, as it gives them ideas for their own performance and also enables them to ask critical questions.

Resources: in role-play situations access to relevant props is important as this makes it more meaningful and enjoyable. Usually schools have basic props but, if not, an art session before the activities can be used to make the props. Role-play activities without any props are doomed to fail. Teaching assistants often have good ideas about producing props.

Plenary

Plenaries are important for exploring children's ideas and feelings about hospitals as well as their views about others in the play. Ask them to think about relevant questions they would like to ask each other. The discussions are meant to challenge stereotypical ideas about how people who may not speak English are treated in hospitals.

Activity Two

The next exercise is planned to develop children's oracy and collaborative skills further by presenting more challenging scenarios. The content of the role-play may depend on the individual teacher. It can be an extension of the hospital scenario but shift to another ward to explore the issue of differential treatment of patients and children's ideas about how to ensure fairness. Children may themselves create a hospital scenario. Alternatively, the topic could relate to people using different languages. But the setting might be different, for example an airport. Or it could be a play about a religious festival – if the children feel comfortable about using aspects of their own cultures and languages. The possibilities are limitless. The teachers will need to know their pupils' cultural experiences and devise role-play situations accordingly.

Activity 2
Role-play scenario: intercultural marriages
Year group: years 10, 11.

The dilemmas surrounding people from different religious back-grounds who want to get married when their parents are against it and want them to marry someone from their own religion are complex. The issues are sensitive but may well be familiar to the students. If the school already uses techniques like Psychology for Children (Lipman, 1988) or Socratic dialogue (Saran and Neisser, 2004) the students will have a familiar structure within which to work.

Setting the scene: Complex topics such as this need to be ap-proached with sensitivity and carefully planned. The role-play could be an extension of topic work on religions that the students have been working on or a cross curricular topic on citizenship and identity. The preparation stage should be carefully monitored and assessed by the class teacher and wherever possible expert advice be sought from an EMA specialist teacher, possibly plan-ning and delivering the session jointly.

Again, it is essential that the students fully understand the task before they get into their groups to decide how they are going to approach this play. The teacher's role is to offer possibilities rather than conditions for the play, merely presenting the scenario and the 'problem'. Students are free to develop it and come up with their own ideas in their own groups. The teacher will need to check that the roles are all assigned and everyone is happy about their role. Students will have control over how their play is to be organised, developed and delivered.

Complex topics of this type reflect some of the cultural ex-periences of young people and their families. Many students have experienced similar issues within their immediate families or their communities and the different views students bring into the discussion must not be shouted down. Although teachers present solving this issue as a challenge it must be clear that there are no fixed right or wrong answers and whatever solutions students come up with in their plays have to be respected.

Facilitating first language use in role-play

It is fair to assume that older students will not need much encouragement about using their home languages but the teacher will still have to plan for the use of home languages in the activities.

■ Communication between the 'parents' and their 'children' takes place in the home language. This may require either a translator for the audience or be communicated through another actor.

■ The ceremony – if there is going to be one – will be conducted in the home language and the students need to think about and organise this.

■ Suggest possible community scenes such as shopping, festivals or attending a place of worship, where home languages will need to be used.

■ Or suggest scenes where the two families meet and ask students for translations of the conversations which would be in home languages.

The students will have ideas about other suitable scenarios for using both their languages.

Plenary

The main point of plenaries is to sum up key points in the play, gather collective ideas, discuss potentially hazardous situations and, most importantly, give students opportunities to talk about their own interpretations of their roles. The teacher's task is to gather all these ideas and present them in a coherent way. The main points are put on the board and presented to the students as their ideas of possible solutions to the issue.

Teachers will find – as I have done – that such activities provide opportunities for other related work. Written stories can come out of the plays or there could even be a much bigger production organised by the students and assisted by the teacher. In the many drama and role-play activities I have seen in primary and secondary schools, I have been constantly impressed by the level of maturity displayed by the children who are given responsibilities of organising and acting in such presentations.

Such activities can also generate further discussions on how each student felt about their situation in role. Having to reflect on their own thinking and feelings about a certain situation, learners develop a sense of responsibility which boosts their confidence. For bilingual pupils this is a vital approach.

Conclusion

This chapter indicates how using children's cultural experiences as starting points for learning produces positive outcomes for bilingual learners. I have extended the principles of collaborative role-play activities used in the previous chapter to suggest examples outside of shopkeeping and trade. My emphasis is on facilitating the use of both languages interchangeably and simultaneously, starting with several confidence building activities before the pupils tackle the complex role-play scenarios.

9

Bilingual classroom practice: success stories from London schools

This chapter describes three bilingual classrooms where the pupils' culturally related experiences are used to enhance their learning.

Case Study 1
Bilingual Science Lesson: Turkish/English
White Hart Lane Secondary School, North London
Year 10 Class

> '*Bugünkü dersimiz ışınların yansıması, yani ...neydi İngilizcesi..?* (today's lesson is about reflection of light, in other words... what is it in English?)

> (Response from the pupils) 'Reflection'.

> '*Evet aferin çocuklar*'. (Well done, children, reflection).

That was the start of typical day at White Hart Lane School. The lesson was Science and Mr. Dedezade an experienced bilingual science teacher began his lesson by recapping on the children's previous learning. This new project involving teaching national curriculum Science in two languages is already making an impact.

The school and the pupils

White Hart Lane School is situated in Tottenham, North London and has a large majority of Turkish and Kurdish speaking pupils. There is a trend of underachievement and the Bilingual Science Project was set up to reverse this.

The 20 pupils in the class all speak Turkish. They were either born in the UK or came here as infants from rural parts of mainland Turkey. Some could also speak Kurdish and all were literate in Turkish and English. Their families were predominantly in the low socio-economic bracket and the parents had mainly manual/ semiskilled jobs or were small shop owners. Children used Turkish or Kurdish at home as their parents were first generation migrants from Turkey.

Lesson plan, content and structure

The lesson was linked directly to NC programmes of study on light and the way it travels on surfaces. When setting out the learning objectives and his methodology, Mr Dedezade specifically focused on the related tasks, not just for their suitability for meeting the learning objectives but also in terms of specific language demands. These were divided into relevant areas: speaking, reading, writing and key vocabulary, as shown below.

SC4 Physical Processes
AT3 Everyday effects of light

Learning objectives: students will be taught that:

■ Light travels from a source (revisit from last lesson)

■ Light is reflected from surfaces

■ We see things only when light from them enters our eyes

The topic for the day was linked to the pupils' forthcoming GCSE on light and how it travels on various surfaces. Mr. Dedezade had a quick recap on what was covered in the previous lesson, asking key questions. He used both Turkish and English to reinforce key points and explain new concepts. Key vocabulary in the two languages was written on the board and constantly revisited. The success of his approach was linked mainly to this strategy. The class was quite challenging in terms of behaviour. Mr. Dedezade used mainly Turkish, more familiar to his pupils, to diffuse some of the tensions. This had a positive effect on pupils, being more directly personal and perceived as the language of shared experience.

Lesson content and structure

Activity	Whole Class Group/Individual	Language	Key Vocabulary Eng.	Turk
Brainstorming	Whole Class	**Speaking/listening**		
• Recap: what did we learn on Wednesday?		Check if they can repeat key sources	Light / sun	*ışın* / *güneş*
• Repeat sources of light (5min)		Encourage full sentences with key vocabulary	lamp / moon / star	*lamba* / *ay* / *yıldız*
Can you think of any surfaces that reflect light? Discuss with partners. Give examples of personal experience e.g. Turkey/ holiday (5min)	Pairs	**Speaking/listening** Asking/ brainstorming Reporting	mirror / reflection / shiny / polished / metals / iron	*ayna* / *yansıma* / *parlak* / *parlatılmış* / *metaller* / *demir*
Feedback (5min) What did your partner say?	Individual	**Speaking/listening** Reporting	silver / bronze / copper / water	*gümüş* / *bronz* / *bakır* / *su*

Lesson content and structure (continued)

Activity	Whole Class Group/Individual	Language	Key Vocabulary Eng.	Turk.
Main activity How do we see things? Introduction **Demonstration + modelling** Angle of reflections from various surfaces ICT interactive whiteboard	**Whole class**	**Listening** to questions and demonstration **Reading** information and key vocabulary from board **Describing** similar processes/ reflection of things in water e.g. here/holiday in Turkey	light reflection ship sea enter see	*ışın* *yansıma* *gemi* *deniz* *girmek* *görmek*
Group tasks (20 min) Work out the angle of reflections from various surfaces. Would you be able to see these objects? Discuss within groups then carryout the tasks.	**Groups** Differentiated tasks **Extension group:** work out the reflections and draw a few similar ones. **More needy group:** a few finished models presented. Apply the same principle to do more of these. Sit close to the interactive	**Reading** information from sources provided **Discussing** possibilities/trying out various angles **(Tur/Eng) Recording** results. Writing explanations to support findings	narrow wide enter see eyes shadows pass through surface formation	*dar* *geniş* *girmek* *görmek* *gözler* *gölge* *geçmek* *içinden* *yüzey* *oluşum*

Lesson content and structure (continued)

Activity	Whole Class Group/Individual	Language	Key Vocabulary
	– Manipulate angles, surfaces/objects to get the right position – Test by acting out the same positions with children (adult supervision)		
Plenary Reinforce/consolidate	Groups to share findings and demonstrate how they reached their answers – More needy group to demonstrate how they confirmed findings. Teacher to extend by presenting another example with multiple positions. Can we see this?		

The lesson was experimental and very interactive. Each pupil's response was sought for and answers in Turkish and English were given equal weight by the teacher. When a response was made in Turkish, the final explanation was reinforced in English. Turkish was the language that facilitated the ideas and concepts to be communicated and these were then reinforced or clarified in English. The teacher's implicit message was that 'if you don't understand this you will get a chance to hear it in the other language and if you cannot explain it in English, I will also accept an explanation in Turkish.' This raised the level of interaction and fostered an atmosphere of mutual respect between teacher and pupils. The pupils I spoke to afterwards told me how much they had disliked Science before joining Mr. Dedezade's class and how the bilingual lessons transformed their attitude and turned it into a subject they 'rather liked'. When I asked one of the pupils how this came about, she replied: 'Because we can understand it now'. When I asked what it was about the particular lesson which helped her understand it, she replied:

> Sir uses Turkish, but not just any Turkish, it makes sense to us. He makes us feel as if we all know it already and he is just reminding us.

The key to Mr. Dedezade's success was the way he related a particular aspect of reflection to children's everyday experiences as Turkish speaking children growing up in the UK, but also as members of their linguistic community, using Turkish in everyday interactions and being exposed to Turkish media. For example as Mr. Dedezade was describing the process of reflection through water, he switched to Turkish and asked the children to think about the journey they made in a boat while on holiday in Turkey. Chatting stopped immediately and everyone had something to say. Mr. Dedezade allowed all the pupils have their say and linked their personal experiences to a new area of learning, i.e. how it is that the front of the ship appears bent as we see it moving through water. Children were interested because they were learning something new that was presented as a natural extension of their previous experiences.

My conversations with Mr. Dedezade confirmed this approach:

> These children are keen to learn but I think what we often present to them is somehow is seen as totally new and undiscovered so only relevant to the pupils who can manage it. What I try and do

here is to present things as an extension of, or linked to, their own experiences. The key to it in my view is the use of Turkish, their main language at home. It is amazing how they express what was previously hidden in their minds. Turkish here reflects common values and experiences. What I see essentially as my role is to utilise these and convert them to a language of the school which is in Standard English. I essentially see my role as a facilitator.

Case Study 2
Year 7 Maths Lesson in Panjabi/English
Guru Nanak Sikh Secondary School in Hayes

Background information
Guru Nanak Sikh Secondary School is the only maintained Sikh secondary school in the country and probably the only one in Europe. The school has 350 students, the vast majority of whom come from Sikh families. The teaching staff are from diverse multi-ethnic communities.

I had a chance to observe PGCE student Varinder Bakshi plan and deliver a lesson for a class of thirty Year 7 children. Her objective was to teach students to learn how to read numbers 1-20 in Panjabi. The example presented here is used to demonstrate how to use children's stronger language, in this case English, to support the learning of the second, Panjabi.

The lesson objectives were linked to the NC Maths Programmes of Study. The plan was based on full pupil participation through interactive games and visual support. It was well differentiated for the different abilities in the class.

One of the strengths of this lesson was the richness of the differentiated resources the student teacher used and her ability to engage children's interest by means of the games, with their colourful symbols and shapes. What interested the children and consequently inspired their learning was the variety of activities planned and delivered by Ms. Bakshi. The whole class *Bingo* activity shown in the chart followed group activities to encourage partnership work and were further reinforced by another set of group activities. The differentiated worksheets also catered for variations within each ability group, so each child could tackle an appropriate task and move on to the next activity. In each task the children were sufficiently challenged. This meant that the student

Lesson structure

Objective of the lesson	• learn how to read numbers 1-20 (NC Ma2-Number and Number system)
	• recognise the symbols of numbers
Introduction (10 min)	• welcome pupils into class
	• do prayer
	• go through flash cards with just numbers written on them
	• pick out 3 good readers to read the numbers
	• ask children of they see any pattern with the sequence
Main Part of the lesson (30 min)	• hold up flash cards with numbers and images on them
	• go through flash cards which have images only
	• discuss the images. Ask the children if they know what the images are of in Panjabi.
	• point out the symbols
	• go though the number cards that have no pictures
	• hand out the number only cards in the wrong order and ask the children to make a human number line
	• carry out some mathematical equations with the number line
	• ask questions in Panjabi, such as:

1. how old are you?

2. how many people are in your family?

3. what is your shoe size?

Lesson structure (continued)

	4. how many sisters do you have?
	5. how many brothers do you have?
	Children are to respond by showing their answers with their number lines
Group Activities 1	Complete differentiated worksheets **Core group**: match numbers to symbols **Lower ability**: work on support sheet with symbols corresponding number of dots (e.g. number 7, opposite 7 dots) **Higher ability**: can you make up any beyond 20 using the support sheet provided (symbols/matching numbers)
Paired work	**Bingo game** Teacher shows a symbol or a number and children who have the corresponding number or symbol show theirs.
Group Activities 2	**Core group**: cut out and match written numbers to number of dots not given in order) **Lower ability**: cut out and match written numbers to dots (numbers given in order) **Higher ability**: to complete more equations on the sheet.
Plenary	• Distribute number fans, one to be shared between two students • Call out a number and have the pupils hold up the number fan that has the number called out

teacher could evaluate their abilities at each task but also that progression was facilitated by a logical and coherent pattern to learning. The activities were enjoyable for the children and encouraged full class participation as well as collaboration between pupils. The classroom was cramped for thirty children – a recipe for a disruptive lesson. But the nature of the activities enabled the teacher to sustain the children's interest and concentration.

The student teacher's balanced use of the two languages also contributed to the lesson's success. It was about learning Panjabi numbers, but the pupils' stronger language needed to be used in order for them to understand and to enhance their learning. Ms. Bakshi used her English skills to determine the level of the children's understanding and employed it as a useful tool for assessment in the class. For example in the first part of the lesson Ms. Bakshi asked in English 'what's this number in Panjabi?' Or 'how do we say this in Panjabi?' with the object of reinforcing the objectives of the lesson. She skilfully shifted to modelling the same questions in Panjabi so the children used Panjabi more, especially when identifying the numbers. English was used to reinforce learning and clarify matters.

During the activities constant interaction was going on between the student teacher and the pupils. The sequence followed during the main part of the lesson as shown in the chart clearly reveals what strategies were used to facilitate oracy. I interpreted Ms. Bakshi's deliberately putting the numbers in the wrong order as an invitation for the children to talk and debate, and this is what happened. The children began to discuss among themselves where each number should go. There even appeared to be slight confusion about who should go into which group as debate and collaboration continued in both languages. The teacher's questioning technique was helpful in setting the frame of thinking for the children:

Teacher	Why should this (number) be there? (Repeats the question in Panjabi).
Child	Because there is more in that one.
Teacher	OK. Which number comes next do you think? (repeats the question in Panjabi)
	(A child calls out the number in English

Teacher	Good! Who also knows that number in Panjabi'
Child	*Sohlaan* (sixteen)
ST	Good! Let's count them all in Panjabi this time.
	(The whole class counts from 1 to 20 in Panjabi)

The teacher had a plenary session to consolidate what had been covered and to explain children's misconceptions about the symbols. She set further challenges by trying to extend the children's learning beyond 20. The homework set at the end of the lesson was linked to what was covered but also concerned numbers above 20. The children were clearly ready for their next challenge when the bell rang to end of the lesson.

During the lesson I had a chance to talk to some of the pupils. I asked one boy 'Does having a maths lesson in two languages help your understanding?

Pupil	Yes, definitely because I know the numbers in English and this helps me understand Panjabi numbers better'
TI	You mean rather than having it all in Panjabi?
Pupil	Yes, that's it. Because when I was in Panjabi (Saturday) school before sometimes the teacher spoke only in Panjabi, that's hard!

I asked another pupil about the lesson being conducted in two languages:

It's good. It gives us a chance to speak to each other in English and Panjabi as we like. If we get something wrong in one then we use the other to see what it is called. Miss helps us a lot.

One girl said 'It's fun because we work in groups and lot of fun games and stuff!'

Ms. Bakshi agreed:

This is not one of the easiest of classes, that's why I need to plan really well for my lessons and make sure that they have a lot of fun activities which are challenging. They love the number Bingo activity, they always ask me to do it again.

When I asked Ms. Bakshi about using two languages and how that helps learning Panjabi, she said 'apart from a few, for most of them English is the stronger language, so I try and use this as basis for learning other things in Panjabi'. When I asked whether this worked, she replied:

> Yes, provided this approach is supported by interactive, visual activities which are fun and encourage collaboration, children enjoy working in groups and learn together, provided of course the groups are carefully selected.'

It appears that just having a lesson in two languages does not automatically make it successful. One needs the ingredients required for any lesson: namely well-planned, structured and interactive delivery of a topic which uses children's experiences as a starting point for learning. In the Panjabi Maths lesson, the children's linguistic experiences in Panjabi and English were the basis for their learning. They were encouraged to use both languages freely throughout the activities. This enhanced their understanding and balanced out the power relationships between members by giving opportunities to those who were more comfortable with using one language or the other in particular situations. The output was in Panjabi but the process was two-way bilingual interaction. This approach contributed to a cohesive atmosphere in the classroom. Overall it was the student teacher's modelling of the use of the two languages which brought home the message:

> We are learning about numbers in Panjabi but we will do so by first exploring what we know in a medium more familiar to us.

It was clear that in bilingual classrooms two or more languages can co-exist for their mutual benefit. How and when each was used will vary according to the context of learning in the classroom. For example, there is nothing more natural than asking children to use Panjabi to describe their experiences at a Panjabi wedding in the UK. Equally, it is acceptable that the child use English to describe some of the more English features of those experiences, such as meeting a friend from school there and what they did together at the party.

The children's language choice may also be influenced by their thinking and this is reflected in their choice of repertoire in a particular context. In such situations children often ask questions such as 'What's the best way to describe this?' The Panjabi Maths lesson was not just about expressing what children could say in the best way they could say it but also to use what they could say to learn to say things in a different way. What we call good teaching is essentially creating opportunities for children to use their linguistic repertoires for learning new things. This particular lesson was an excellent example.

Case study 3:

'Let's buy some shalwaar': Panjabi children's role-play in a shop transaction process.

Guru Gobind Kahalsa Panjabi School

The final case study comes from Guru Gobind Khalsa College in Essex, where I observed a primary Year 3 class. The activity was an extension of the children's ongoing work on shops and money transactions between customers and shopkeepers. I was not present at the lesson but the class teacher kindly video-recorded the activity for my benefit and spoke to me beforehand and afterwards.

Background information on the school

■ Guru Gobind Khalsa College is a successful independent Sikh school, one of the highest performing schools in the area. The key to its success is its multicultural ethos. Although it is predominantly Sikh in character, children from other faiths also attend the school. The use of all languages is openly encouraged and

■ there is a positive atmosphere in the school. The school succeeds in utilising children's languages, linking them to their understanding and use of Standard English.

The class and the project

A Year 3 class was working on a project on shops and the transaction process involving money and customer interaction. They had been looking at the kinds of shops in the locality and exchanging information about the customers and the shopkeepers. The class teacher, who speaks fluent Panjabi, extended the work to a role-play situation set in a Panjabi clothing shop. She was interested to see how far the children's home experiences were reflected and whether this aided their understanding of the transaction process.

Mrs. Simran Dillon explained the scenario to children:

> There is a Panjabi shop that sells salwaar and other types of
> materials. One group will be customers and the other shop
> keepers. The customers should try and get the best deal out of
> their visit and of course be aware that the shopkeepers are after
> making money for themselves, You can set your own prices and
> arrange your shop as you like.

As in many cultures, bargaining is used amongst customers in
Panjabi culture in exchange of goods in shop transaction processes. The children had been exposed to bargaining in their communities and were accustomed to it. The teacher explained that
they were free to decide how they wanted to approach the role-
play. She was keen to see the pupils working out different ideas.
She told them they were free to use English and Panjabi but reminded them that they were running or visiting a Panjabi shop.
First she put the children into groups and defined their roles as
shopkeepers or customers and asked them to decide what they
were going to do – for example customers should agree how hard
they would push their luck before finally buying an item. The shop
owners had different concerns: Should they arrange their shops,
who would do what? What prices would they charge and what was
the limit of such prices to be? Children were given half an hour to
discuss and sort things out in their groups.

In the sample extract opposite three boys are given the role of
shopkeepers and are visited by three girls.

We can already see the children engaging with the role-play. The
shopkeepers are eager to please their customers and the customers
are already expecting the shopkeepers to satisfy them. The teacher
assured me that none of this had been rehearsed, but the children
had been carefully briefed about their roles. They felt comfortable
in these roles, having been exposed to such routine shop transactions within their communities. Notice that the conversation
was solely in Panjabi in this section, even though there were no
restrictions on what language could be used. But as they saw it,
this was Panjabi shop selling salwaar so the activity could only be
communicated in Panjabi.

The children brought in many different kinds of Panjabi fabrics
and made their shops look as convincing as possible. In this
extract two boys, shopkeepers Ajay and Akam, are visited by three
customers who seem unable to decide what they want. The shopkeepers are keen to show what is available but they also display

Utter. No.	Name of Child/ren	Remarks	Utterance	Translation
1	Akam Ajay		*Akal phaji, sat sri Akal phenji*	Hello brother Hello sister
2	Prabhjeet		*Sat sri akal*	Hello
3	Pawan		*Kee haal hai?*	How are you?
4	Akam		*Fus Kalas Kee chayella?*	I am great What do you want?
5	Pawan		*Salwaar chadi ya*	I want Salwaar
6	Akam	(to Ajay)	*Acha, jao, thusi daso*	Go and show them
7	Ajay		*Al Walee?*	This one?
8	Prabhjeet		*Nehin*	No
9	Akam		*Al walee?*	This one?
10	Prabhjeet		*Nehin*	No
11	Ajay		*Ah walee, ah walee pher*	This one how about this one?
12	Prabhjeet		*Haan*	Yes
13	Ravjyot		*Nehin*	No
14	Prabjeet		*Nehin*	No
15	Akam		*Al walee, eh chooti jahi*	This one this small one
16	Prabhjeet		*Nehin Ahaa, aha Bahut diamond*	No This one, this one loads of diamonds

much patience with their customers. And eventually customers see something they like and decide to go for it. The bargaining begins.

The heated debate continued. The shopkeepers were determined to sell something to their customers. There were a lot of possibilities for buying and selling things, and both parties expected this to happen. There was no explicit demand for preferential treatment by the customers. The shopkeepers did not question things either, patiently attending to customers, although some did

Utter. No	Name of Child/ren	Remarks	Utterance	Translation
18	Pawan		*Eh Wali kehnay dhi ah?*	How much is this one?
19	Akam		*Ah wali? Ehh 25 pounds dhi*	That one? Is 25 pounds
20	Prabhjeet		*Menghi hai!*	Its expensive!
21	Ajay	(quickly showing another one)	*Eh..20 pounds?*	This one is 20 pounds
22	Pawan		*Ah bahut menghi hai*	That one is too expensive
23	Akam		*Low cost 15 pounds shi kurdahar ghay*	We will give it to you at low cost for 15 pounds.
24	Ajay	(sensing the opportunity)		fifteen
25	Navnjeet		*1 K pound hai!*	It's one pound!
26	Prabhjeet		*1K pound hai!*	It's one pound!
27	Akam	(outraged)	*Ik pound nehin eh? Best price ten pound. Dhi dhegyungsu(?)*	It's not one pound! We will give it to you for the best price ten pounds!
29	Navnjeet	(to Akam)	*Tapar marani ghei!*	I will slap you!
30	Akam		*Thelmo chaydhi eh chuni 5 pound dhi?*	Do you want this scarf, it is 5 pounds

occasionally lose their cool (Navnjeet line 29). All were accepted the given rules of the game.

The children often accompany their parents to shops of this kind and witness the bargaining that goes on. The transcripts capture the manifestation of these experiences as extensions of their real life experiences.

The use of Panjabi as the language of cultural experiences was crucial to the role-play. It has a specific use here: it is the language of negotiation and bargaining and it appeared to be used in all its aspects: intonation, gestures, sentence construction and specific vocabulary that would reflect the mood of the commercial exchange. The children did use certain English vocabulary in their interactions. They might substitute English words when they did not remember the Panjabi, such as *pound,* or choose a phrase they found appropriate, such as *low cost* (line 23).

Planning and organising the tasks

The activity was planned to facilitate children's oral language skills in a collaborative group context. At the start of the video, we see a perfectly organised shop with clothing arranged tidily across neat 'stalls' (tables set out in a circle) and a group of boys and girls causing havoc in it until broken up by the teacher's gentle: 'OK! Lets start now!' Children quickly organise themselves into customers/shopkeepers and prepare for action.

The level of excitement observed at the beginning of the video appeared to conceal the debating, arguing and the high level of communication between the groups before the game began. Children were given a task: as customers they were to debate the range of strategies they were going to use in order to accomplish maximum profit by obtaining the lowest price on each item – which they expected the shopkeepers to have to reduce. There were many items: shalwars, diamond designed shawls, saris etc. The price for each had to be negotiated collectively as success depended upon a unified front with regard to prices. It was the only way to persuade the shopkeepers to reduce the prices. The shopkeepers were discussing counter tactics. How prepared were the customers likely to be? How much did they set their limit of what they would pay? How far could they try their luck? Children debated, challenged each other's ideas and finally agreed a strategy to deal with the customers. They used Panjabi and English sentences freely in their discussions, exchanging ideas in one and switching half way through to the other or even borrowing single words and phrases. The end result was that the children generated interesting suggestions with the help of their enriched vocabulary.

In the shopkeepers' corner

Akam	*eh wali Keynay dhi ah* (how much is this one?
Ajay	Let make it twenty- five!
Akam	No! it's too expensive, they won't buy it!
Ajay	*Eh* twenty *dhi* then! (Its twenty pounds then)
Akam	OK. Low cost fifteen pounds *kurdhan ghay* (OK we will give it at low cost fifteen pounds)

Similar debates were going on in the customers' corner:

Pawan	OK gang! What prices should we ask for?
Prabhjeet	Let's make their lives a misery. Ask for a very low price.
Pawan	They won't fall for it.
Navnjeet	OK. Shall we just be silly and get on their nerves.
Prabhjeet	How?
Navnjeet	Get them to give us the prices of all the items one by one, *then* (her emphasis) suggest a silly price.
Pawan	Yes! then they will say its impossible, then we will say bit higher price.

It is reasonable to assume that such sophistication in their thinking is not due merely to the children's learning in the classroom. The confidence displayed by these girls suggests an accumulation of culturally related experiences of shop transactions. Customer masterminds are at work, carefully devising a strategy to fool the shop owners. There is a strong sense of decentralised thinking that challenges Piagetian notions of development stages. In carefully organised classroom learning contexts, children can develop their thinking through the use of their languages (Vygotsky, 1978). The role of the teacher in facilitating a classroom environment that allows this to happen is crucial.

The class teacher spoke about her thinking when she designed the activity.

I began my conversation with Mrs. Dillon by asking her about her perception of her role in an activity of this kind. 'I essentially see my role as one of a facilitator' she told me. She continued:

MD   All children but especially the bilingual children need to be given opportunities to use their oral skills in both languages.

TI   Why do you think this is so important?

MD   Because I feel that both languages carry the linguistic representations of various experiences in their minds, and often children are not aware that they actually possess these through two language mediums. They rather see the two languages as separate and often not related. I think this is because children do not often have many opportunities to use them together to establish a linguistic interrelationship. I think that through carefully constructed and challenging scenarios children can be given the opportunities to use their linguistic skills orally through collaborative group activities.

TI   The video showed clearly the intensity of collaboration and debate.

MD   These children live through these experiences every day of their lives in their communities and it was an opportunity for them not just to debate these but orally to sound out their ideas and by listening to others, but most importantly to test the impact of their own thinking in relation to others in the group. This, I think, is the key recipe for further learning.

TI   How does a bilingual medium help the learning process do you think? Can you tell me a bit about that?

MD   Giving the children the opportunity to use their linguistic repertoires opens up two linguistic channels for interaction. This creates enormous possibilities for the use of vocabulary, key phrases and sentences. Apart from this it gives children further opportunities to take more chances with their own ideas, as having two channels will provide more freedom of choice of vocabulary related to key concepts – hence the production of wonderfully arranged sentences rich with borrowings and switches. When this is achieved, i.e. once children discover that they can express themselves and their ideas more effectively, then this opens up enormous new possibilities for the development of new ideas and will gradually result in more risk taking with their own ideas. This is the beginning of the process called 'new learning'. I haven't even talked about the benefits of being exposed to other models of speech (or ideas) from other children within the group. It is an exciting process.

Going back to your earlier question relating to my role, I simply plan the activity and clearly set out the learning outcomes, e.g. to be able to devise a number of cost related strategies in buying or selling. However, I allow children to develop it for themselves, occasionally coming in to provide some direction and prompt them with some key questions. I usually do this not by just coming in and disrupting the flow of the play but presenting myself as a customer or a shop keeper, and children are quite receptive to that. They know who I am and accept me into their game. It makes things a bit more fun then. Essentially, I see the activities as a source of challenges and I think this is the key to learning: to force children's existing boundaries of thinking. I felt I have achieved some of it here, however I am aware that some other areas of my work remains to be developed further. There were two visible aspects of this activity which I regard as positive. One was an almost simultaneous increase in the level of language use (both Panjabi and English) and the level of interaction between the children. The second was their happy smiling faces as they were playing the game.

The evidence from the video as well as the transcripts fully confirmed Mrs. Dillon's views.

10

Children's understanding of culturally related concepts

The primary focus of this book is to explore approaches to teaching which specifically meet the needs of Turkish speaking children in the UK. My objective is educational. I tried to develop specific teaching approaches to take account of their history, culture and life in London. However, I quickly became aware that the agenda was not purely educational, that one's own view of oneself as part of a community and one's own identity carry political connotations. This book has examined how language is interwoven with distinct cultural experiences and how these can be used to support teaching and learning in the classroom.

The book shows how the socio-economic experiences of the families of Turkish speaking children affect the children's learning in bilingual collaborative settings. It is clear that children's thinking relating to economic concepts can be varied and depends upon a multiplicity of factors concerning their cultural experiences, particular learning contexts and the development that comes with maturity. Using the language through which such experiences are developed, negotiated and communicated positively affects children's economic understanding.

We saw how the development of economic concepts depends on each child's interpretation of their learning environment. Development is both a social and an individual process. The view that social forces act on an individual, who is positioned as a passive recipient, is contradicted by the children's discourses shown here.

Investigating children's understanding of cost by seeing how they priced the goods in their stores proved to be quite complex. Their negotiations showed that the price of an item could mean a variety of things: it could mean the selling price of items they thought very hard about pricing so as to make profit. But the price of an item could also be varied according to circumstances – the children discovered that prices could be changed when doing so would keep their existing customers and prevent losses. At other times prices had to remain fixed to keep existing customers.

Children also showed more than a simple understanding about money. They all knew that money was needed to buy things from their own stores, from the wholesaler or from stores they visited. The children were also aware of the different currencies used in England and Cyprus, although they were not sure of their relative value. Some children even showed understanding of the uses of money beyond that of exchange – that it could be used to pay people to work in their stores and for buying stock or services.

To the children buying could mean buying from either a wholesaler or a rival store. When buying from a wholesaler, children showed awareness of several interrelated variables. The prices charged by the wholesaler affected their own selling prices as well as how many items they could buy. The children knew they needed to be careful about buying from the rival store, as their buying power depended upon the money they made in their own stores and this was linked to the number of customers visiting their stores. Some of the children understood the connection between pricing and how much they paid the wholesaler at the beginning, whereas others could not perceive the complex relationships operating in transactions.

Children attached a variety of meanings to this conceptual area of work. They knew that work involved sharing collective responsibilities. During the initial pricing and labelling activities, children were able to organise the routine tasks successfully as a group. When asked to negotiate a division of responsibilities in their truck company, they managed to do so quite successfully, especially the girls. The girls showed sophistication and maturity in their responses to the boys, challenging their dominant behaviour while endorsing their acceptable roles as drivers. The girls were team builders and knew that effective teams need members who work in harmony. Their approach was inclusive; they challenged the boys only until the boys were willing to play the game properly, and they adopted an inclusive strategy.

All the children in the study showed some understanding of the issues concerning cost, buying, money and work. But they showed different levels of understanding about each financial aspect. For example, one of the storekeepers, Şefik, knew that the price charged by his own store had to be greater than the price charged by the wholesaler (Extract 7.1.2). Yet despite hearing that an item was sold cheaper in another store, he did not make any attempt to change the price offered to a customer in his store, so missed out on the potential profits to be made from the customer's visit. However, it was Şefik who took a leading role in editing the relevant sections of a bilingual newspaper and made impressively useful suggestions (Extract 7.1.3).

With the exception of one storekeeper, Banu, none of the children showed any understanding of the variable factors in buying (see chapter 6) and it was only Banu and Binnur who showed understanding of money beyond that of exchange (chapter 5, section 3).

This strengthens my argument that although children shared cultural experiences they do not necessarily develop particular levels of understanding at the same time. The children in this study came from home environments where their parents owned small businesses and all had spent time in their stores. Sometimes they helped their parents with routine tasks in them such as carrying or tidying things. They had opportunities to observe transaction in the stores and were also exposed to talk about the business of shopkeeping at home. Although one cannot predict how much such experiences influence children's understanding, I expected that the children would show some common areas of thinking across the economic areas explored. But this was seldom the case; more often there were marked differences in their understanding of concepts.

Moreover the age of the child did not necessarily correlate with their understanding of a concept. Some of the children in this study, who fell within the age categories defined by stage theorists, failed to show the understanding of certain concepts which the stage theorists would expect. Take the findings about profit: it was not their ages but whether they had experience of shopkeeping that determined who showed greater understanding. This suggests that not all children go through a universal stage in their understanding of economic concepts and that there appears to be no direct connection to age.

So it seems that other factors might influence children's understanding of economic concepts. One appeared to be how the activities organised in the classroom facilitated the children's interaction. As they debated and discussed an activity in role, some children's understanding changed significantly. They became more prudent with their money, and began making complex logical decisions about lowering or raising prices. They were clearly aware of multiple variables when they were buying from a wholesaler, as Binnur and Funda show in their response to buying from the wholesaler (extract 7.1.2).

In each conceptual area, the level of communication between the children and their organisation of the identified activities increased. They established collaboration by negotiating terms in role. The increase in the level of collaboration was not achieved by one member of the group becoming dominant. Difficulties that arose were often solved by collaborative approaches by the girls. These approaches helped achieve positive working relationships in each team. The groups became helpful and supportive, often giving and taking advice from each other. Children who had hung back initially increased their participation, particularly in activities that appeared to link with their particular cultural experiences. Children gained by participating in the activities because of the positive collaboration in the group.

The children began interacting much more and discussing the tasks more openly among themselves. They became more tolerant of each other's suggestions. The tasks were planned to be increasingly demanding, and my intervention in role lessened as the activities progressed, leaving the children to organise themselves and make their own decisions. In contrast to the earlier activities, their increased interaction was conducted in both their languages, which they used more frequently and interchangeably.

We saw how children's interactions in situations in which two languages were used interchangeably increased their use of economic related vocabulary. This is not to claim that the economic vocabulary was a natural consequence of bilingual interaction – it is the transactions that were more conducive to language production. When Binnur and Emine discussed various aspects of fixing prices, they used Turkish and English interchangeably. Clearly there needs to be a meaningful context for interaction that is conducive to the use of both languages, to stimulate the production of relevant vocabulary. The store activities created a natural environment in which to speak both languages.

The children's conversations in which they considered multiple variables in buying from a wholesaler showed how they reflect on their previous actions and re-evaluate their thinking. My findings fit with other studies on bilinguals' performing better than their monolingual peers in flexibility, fluency, originality and elaboration in thinking. The ability of children in one of the stores in this study, to analyse the variables affecting the prices supports this view, as do children's positive responses to conversations I initiated (see extract 7.1.3).

It was partly my own investigation of various approaches to teaching that made me begin looking at models of good classroom practice, for example collaborative activities that gave children opportunities to talk and listen to each other. I was seeking bilingual classroom practices which would specifically support my point about the positive correlation between culturally specific experiences and the bilingual classroom contexts. The activities and suggestions selected in chapter 8 were guided by the principle that bilingual contexts of learning planned and delivered in collaborative group interaction contexts enhance learning. As I discussed in my findings, the content of teaching was an important dimension. To use what children experience in their everyday community activities provided the main focus for the three bilingual lessons I presented in chapter 9. These activities were specifically chosen to represent the implications of the findings of the project for the classroom.

The bilingual science lesson was a good example of effective delivery of a subject, framed within the structures of the national curriculum. It was a useful reminder that even the most formal and structured subjects can be delivered within the framework proposed here. What made the science lesson interesting was that it was delivered in two languages and linked to natural things around the home environment. Mr Dedezade, the bilingual science teacher, observed that 'Even on some occasions when we tell children off in Turkish they show a different response, they actually take notice, almost surprised by it all'. In his lesson that afternoon, he hardly used that strategy. He didn't need to. He was interacting constantly with his pupils. His comments were inviting participation and the children took part willingly. For each new concept, vocabulary was linked to an existing concept to the or children's everyday experiences and the vocabulary entailed. Ideas were at once both compared and familiarised using two language mediums. The teacher's approach to teaching science was to make new learning a natural extension of existing knowledge. He spoke to the children in a language which was part of their everyday natural environment. It helped that Mr. Dedezade was himself familiar with the children's cultural experiences.

The interactive Maths lesson is another example of culturally specific teaching and learning. It was fun too. The unfamiliar was tackled through a carefully planned sequence of interesting games. The children had to collaborate in groups to tackle the challenges presented. 'You can use any language you like' said Ms. Bakshi, 'any language that will help you understand each other better'. Naturally, children used their more familiar language, English, to assess and debate things. The end result was mutually beneficial in terms of language learning: to read and write numbers in Panjabi, using what they already knew in English and Panjabi. The other strength of this lesson was that planning was linked to previous learning and the learning outcomes were achievable and had a specific language focus. Key vocabulary linked to specific concepts in both languages emerged.

The Panjabi clothing shop as shown in the third example was set up as a counterpoint to the Turkish shop experience. The children were given a set of challenging tasks which required active group participation. Their home experiences of bargaining were at the core of this challenge: The teacher set children a task: *how could they negotiate a better deal for themselves?* and the children rose to the challenge. The key word *negotiation* was the focus point for interaction. The children debated the strategies and then had a chance to test them as customers and shopkeepers. The language of interaction was Panjabi but it was used interchangeably with English. The children were essentially given the responsibility, with guidance on how to decide what to do and how to go about interpreting their roles. How to do the latter did not require much thinking on their part – it was more of a matter of improvisation. The children enjoyed this activity, finding it different from their routine maths sessions or circle time. The social dimension of learning was also apparent. The collective negotiation of ideas in two language mediums and the equal right of everyone to speak their views in the language of their choice provided context for the development of democratic values and citizenship.

The important ingredients that make a lesson successful are clear. It is well-planned and delivered. The methods of delivery have, in my experience, involved highly visual resources delivered through an interactive and interesting medium. Children are motivated and also enjoy themselves.

As in the case of all successful lessons, the evaluation of the learning outcomes is crucial to planning and progression in learning. In all three examples discussed in this book, the teachers organised their approach to learning well. In all, the teachers' questioning strategies were not just to guide the children in their tasks but also to enable the teachers to assess their pupils' learning – as the teachers themselves stressed. The main concern for the teachers was the impact of their lesson on all the children. 'The biggest challenge for me is how to improve my methods of differentiation' said one. 'There are a variety of abilities in my class'. The others stressed the importance of creating culturally relevant and interesting games to appeal to their pupils' interest and motivate them to engage with the lesson.

All three teachers were agreed that if they as teachers manage to involve their children in a lesson, there is a good chance that learning will take place. I was particularly interested in the teachers' comments about the bilingual contexts of learning. Bilingual themselves, they did not need to be convinced of the obvious benefits of using two language mediums in learning. One sums up the essence of this book:

> Some colleagues quite understandably get a bit apprehensive when there is a mention of using two languages in the classroom. But what I also discovered in these activities is that this is not actually necessary. I mean, it is not absolutely paramount that the

teachers speak both languages. Teaching should be about creating opportunities for children to speak their languages in the framework of carefully planned learning outcomes. It is about empowering children to take an active part in their own learning based on mutual respect. Children are honest. They can be trusted to translate their own thinking into different language mediums for the benefit of others around them. (Ms. Dillon)

So far I have discussed my project findings and their implications for the classrooms and presented three models of bilingual teaching to support them. But what are the implications of my findings for schools and classroom teachers generally? I argue that to facilitate children's learning further, strategies need to be in place at classroom and school levels.

Working with Turkish speaking communities

■ **Classroom level**: teachers need to be well informed about the local Turkish speaking communities and the children's experiences at home and in their supplementary schools.

■ School level: schools need to develop dialogue and ways of collaborating with the local Turkish speaking communities.

All this can be done in a number of different ways. Schools should facilitate certain events, such as international festivals and days of celebrations, inviting members of the communities not just to participate but actually to organise these events in the school. It is astonishing how much response is generated from parents who are told by the school that an event needs to be organised and that expert advice is needed about organising it. For example I recall a remarkable response to a call by one school in Hackney to International Children's Day (23 April). This is the day that was given to all children by Kemal Atatürk to celebrate their contribution to the future of the Turkey. It has since been adopted by all the nations of the world and is celebrated every year. Turks take great pride in this event and even the least active parents willingly give their time to plan and organise it.

The Hackney parents were asked to organise the event with full backing from the school and it became a useful point of discussion between parents and teachers. As the class teachers queried things about the festival, they became more familiar with the parents and with how their pupils lived at home. The information the teachers obtained about the children's home experiences proved useful for planning work in the classroom. For example, the festival would be a good starting point for developing work for history, looking at geographical areas within Turkey as well as other related work about the country, such as festivals and celebrations.

Mini-projects can be developed in which regular visits are made to local community shops and businesses to observe how shops are run. Children could be 'workers' for an hour and get a feel of what it's like to be a shopkeeper. Older children could be organised to work longer, as part of their work experience. Such collaboration could be developed as a class or whole school project, the progression and development being carefully monitored by the teachers and reported regularly in school assemblies. The end of year project can be presented as a mini exhibition with all the achievements and related work proudly displayed for the parents and the community. Schools need to organise such projects with the local communities and seek their active support. An open invitation – with a mention of music – often attracts good attendance from the local community. Parents and the communities need to feel ownership of such projects organised by the schools.

Another useful link is with supplementary schools. A significant majority of Turkish speaking children attend supplementary schools, mainly on Saturdays and some on Sundays. They provide a wealth of experience which can serve as extension activities for the mainstream classrooms such as culturally specific role-play, the physical landscape of Cyprus and Turkey, people and their customs, language and so on. Such activities provide a natural transition into mainstream activities. Certain of the school's teachers may visit and report on the activities that link school projects with the supplementary schools' work. Any visitor to supplementary schools will find that many areas of work covered there are relevant to what is being taught in the mainstream schools. It should only require a few arranged visits over a term to enable teachers to agree the areas to be covered and to set up a medium term plan jointly with the supplementary schools.

Visiting teachers should be given time in lieu for the time they spend in supplementary schools. Joint training days, involving staff from both schools, are valuable on matters like teaching approaches, class management and the national curriculum. These would be facilitated by the mainstream school management teams and built into the school development plan. Such initiatives need to be organised in the context of clear and consistent school policies on communicating and working with parents and encouraging home school partnerships over particular learning objectives on planned activities such as a shop project, homework or visits to the country of origin.

Receiving Turkish speaking newcomers into the school

■ **Classroom level**: full participation in classroom activities can only be achieved by full integration of newcomers – often Kurdish speaking – into the classroom. Class teachers should have established strategies for making new arrivals welcome and accepted into the peer group, such as a buddy system. Class teachers should ensure that children understand the classroom activities and their role in the classroom.

■ **School level**: schools should have effective induction procedures for new pupils, especially those who are new to English and/or refugees from conflict areas. And schools should ensure that key information about new pupils is collected and communicated to all relevant members of staff and used constructively.

The assessment procedures used by the school should take into account the possibility of traumatic experiences and for children who are new to English should be mostly in their first language. LEAs should provide information on qualified professionals who can carry out these assessments.

Raising expectations of Turkish speaking pupils

■ **Classroom level**: teachers should assess the impact of expectations on Turkish speaking children's achievement, particularly

– how pupils' expectations and belief about their own ability as learners affect their achievement

– how teachers' expectations influence pupils' views of their own potential

– how pupils form their views about teachers' expectations of them

– how teachers can balance their concern not to discourage pupils by occasionally setting tasks they know are difficult for them so as to establish high expectations for future achievement.

Productive communication with pupils will give them opportunities to reflect upon their learning and judge how best to improve on their targets, which need to be realistic and achievable. It is about the teacher's own ability to communicate the challenge of set tasks and the pupil's ownership of them.

Also to be considered is assessment. Teachers need to use all available forms of assessment to obtain an accurate picture of the child's strengths and areas of development. As so many Turkish and Kurdish speaking children use Turkish or Kurdish as their first language, it is important that this is used as a tool in assessing them. Assessment should be designed to determine the individual needs of children rather than the average ability in the class. The planned tasks should be

- differentiated to meet the varying needs of bilingual pupils

- provide opportunities for children to use their first language, such as drama activities, telling stories

- interactive with plenty of visual support provided, for example a music lesson with Turkish instruments or appropriate pictures and artefacts

- resources should reflect children's home experiences, for example in a lesson on food, children should be able to handle the food bought from shops

- have clear and specific targets for developing and extending children's language skills. This implies that in addition to the learning outcomes of each lesson, teachers should have specific targets for language acquisition and development. For example if the learning outcome of the lesson is to describe the actions of the characters in the story, I found that asking children to reflect on their own knowledge of adjectives in Turkish motivates them to participate fully. So teachers need to know the linguistic repertoires of their pupils and be trained to focus on this need.

The assessment strategies should be formative, summative, varied and ongoing. Ongoing assessment relates to evaluating the impact of each lesson as it is delivered and should focus on groups as well as a whole class. It can specifically relate to learning outcomes and be recorded in a simple observation sheet. By ticking the related knowledge or skill to be acquired for that particular lesson, the teacher can monitor the impact of each lesson, set realistic targets and plan for the next one. For example if the child is to form grammatically correct sentences, the teacher ticks the relevant box but if they have difficulties in writing, this is specified so the teacher can plan for this the next session. The summative assessment gives the teacher an overall picture of how the child is progressing. The whole school assessment policy will determine whether it is four-weekly, half-termly or termly. In the formative tests prepared by the teacher at the end of each term to evaluate children's progress, the language used should reflect the natural, interactive language she uses in the classroom. This helps to familiarise the task for the children, especially those new to English. The language of the test should take account of culturally specific vocabulary, difficult expressions or idiomatic language and these should be clarified for the whole class.

School level: Schools should have clear procedures for target setting and specific activities in the classroom for raising pupils' expectations. In some successful schools this is done through teachers brainstorming ideas and sharing them with the rest of the staff, generating a wealth of practical activities which can be collected in a handbook for all the staff. Such strategies should be revised regularly at staff training days.

Children are complex and classrooms are complex places. To implement the strategies suggested here requires effective planning and coordination. With their increasing administrative responsibilities, teachers need assistance in carrying out these strategies. The role of Teaching Assistants (TAs) is vital. Regular weekly planning sessions and daily short briefing sessions ensure that TAs are clear about the learning outcomes of each lesson as well as the specific targets for the pupil/s. TAs can also assist with assessment tasks and during whole class sessions they can provide important information relating to particular pupils' responses to the demands of the lesson, reporting who asked questions, what type of questions and how often – or whose responses supported the understanding of the learning outcomes and who said nothing. This gives the teacher an overall picture of each child's progress over a period of time, thus supporting planning and target setting.

In sum, the activities suggested in this book are intended as a framework for class teachers to build on. Each class will have its unique character and pupils with distinctive interests and cultural experiences. It is up to each class teacher to decide how they go about assessing, discovering and capitalising on their learners' strengths and use them to improve their access to learning. This book has shown that teaching approaches which specifically take into account Turkish speaking children's cultural experiences as well as their language skills in collaborative, interactive, role-playing, bilingual and problem solving situations result in their increased participation and increases their language use, so enhancing their learning. Models were suggested of whole school and classroom systems that made this happen effectively.

The ideas explored in this book fall within the discipline of critical psychology. I have argued against the traditional views of developmental psychology, stressing the importance of the wide variety of factors that contribute to a child's conceptual development. I showed that children, as active learners, constantly interact and make sense of the world around them. Children construct their versions of their environment out of the range of experiences they bring to a situation. As we have seen, they constantly negotiate and position themselves in relation to those around them. Learning is essentially a social activity. Children critically evaluate their positions in relation to others, so constructing knowledge and consequently advancing their own development.

Appendix

Extract 4.1.3

81 Emine	How much are you gonna sell this for Banu?	
82 Göksel	What! That! What's this?	
83 Emine (Does not quite remember Göksel's name)	*Ayran!* How much you gonna say you want Döksel for now?	(Ayran – A Turkish yoghurt drink)
84 Göksel	It's not Döksel it's Göksel!	
85 Banu	Anyway. What's this?	
86 Göksel	It's ice cream dumbo!	
87 Banu (annoyed)	I don't see anything alright. I haven't ever seen ice cream on it.	
88 Emine	I have in Germany!	
89 Göksel	I had it eating in the opera!	
90 Emine	One pound! This ice-cream is one pound!	
91 Göksel	Yeah. I know!	
92 Emine (calling Banu)	Banu!	
(showing an item)	One pound?	
93 Banu	How about twenty p!	
94 Göksel	No!	
95 Emine	Just one pound!	
96 Göksel	Because it was just one pound in opera.	

Transcript A (Store 2 – Cappodocia): 81- 96 Emine, Göksel, Banu

Extract 4.3.1

71 Researcher		*Ben geçen hafta gelmiştim, bana büyük sattınız.*	I came last week. You sold me big ones.
72 Funda	(anticipating the complaint)	*E...Birazcık çıktı parası*	Ehm. The price has gone up a bit.
73 Researcher		*Niye böyle ansızın yükselttiniz?*	Why have you brought it up suddenly?
		Diğer tarafta bir dükkan var, onlar büyükleri beş pound'a satıyorlar.	There is a store on the other side, they sell theirs for five pounds.
74 Binnur		*E..biraz para lazım.*	Ehm. We need some money.
75 Researcher		*Fazla almayacağım çünkü bende de para yok.*	I won't be able to buy a lot because I haven't got any money.
76 Funda		Twenty four pounds.	
77 Researcher		Two small ones, are they two pounds each?	
78 Göksel		Yes.	
79 Researcher		I will have two small ones please.	
80 Binnur		The big ones are twenty four and small ones. That will be thirty pounds.	
81 Funda	(sees an approaching customer)	Hello! What would you like?	
82 Şefik		How much are these?	

Extract 4.3.1 (continued)

83 Funda		These? Three pounds.
	(takes the money)	
84 Şefik	(large melon)	How much are these?
85 Funda		Five pounds.
86 Researcher		*Teşekkür ederim..* Thank you.
		İyi işler. Good sales!
87 Banu	(small melon)	How much is that again?
88 Binnur/Funda		Three pounds.

Transcript B (Store 1 – Nicosia): 71-88 Funda, Göksel, Binnur, Şefik, Researcher

Extract 4.2.4

147 Binnur	One thousand because three thousand *karpuz.*	melons
148 Funda	*No! Doküzyüz!*	Nine hundred!
149 Binnur	*No! Sekizyüzelli!*	Eight hundred and fifty!
150 Banu	It's too much. I mean too much water melons.	
151 Binnur	One thousand No! One thousand five hundred. It depends on the thing. On the way it's a lot of things. We will have a price one thousand. If just luggage we will have about five hundred.	

Transcript C: 147-151 Binnur, Banu, Funda

Extract 4.3.2.

36	Binnur		How much is a big one?	
37	Funda		Six pounds.	
38	Binnur		Medium! How do you spell medium?	
39	Şefik		How much are this?	
40	Göksel		Five pounds.	
41	Funda	(to Şefik)	*Sus be!*	Shut up you!
42	Binnur	(whispering to Funda)	Speak Turkish!	
43	Funda		*Ne isten?*	What do you like?
44	Şefik		*Karpuz.*	
45	Funda		*Büyükler altı lira küçükler de üç lira.*	The big ones are six pounds, the small ones are for three.
46	Şefik		*Alırım.*	I'll buy.
47	Funda		*Büyük mü, küçük mü?*	Big ones or small ones?
48	Şefik		*Büyük..*	Big ones.
49	Funda		*Altı lira lütfen.*	Six pounds please.
50	Göksel		I have to give him four pounds change.	
51	Funda	(to Göksel)	You didn't even do it stupid.	

Transcript B (Store 1 – Nicosia): 36-51 Binnur, Şefik, Göksel,Funda,

Extract 4.3.3

45	Researcher	*Büyükler kaç para küçükler kaç para?*	How much are the big ones how much are the small ones?
46	Banu	*Küçükler bir lira, büyükler dört lira.*	Small ones are one pound, big ones are four pounds.
47	Researcher	*Büyükler dört lira mı?*	Are the big ones four pounds?
		Biraz pahalı geldi bana.	It is a bit expensive.
		Orda başka dükkan var,onlar iki pound'a satıyorlar.	There is another store over there, they sell them for two pounds
		O zaman ben yalnız küçük alacağım.	In that case I'll buy only small ones.
48	Emine	How much are the big melons?	
49	Şefik	Ten pounds.	
50	Banu	Four pounds.	
51	Funda	Can I have two big ones please. How much are they?	
52	Banu	Four pounds altogether they are eight pounds.	
53	Funda	Just give me two pounds change thank you. I am not coming to your store again!	
54	Şefik	We don't want you here!	

Transcript B (Store 2 – Cappodocia): 45-54 Banu, Şefik, Emine, Researcher

Extract 5.2.3

287	Göksel		Don't talk in Turkish right?
288	Emine		Hey Banu! Stop doing that.
289	Göksel		*Buranın yirmibes bin lirası beleş!* — Twenty five thousand pound (charged) here is cheap!
290	Emine	(to Göksel)	What?
291	Göksel		*Turkiyenin iki tanesi yok ki!* — There is no two of Turkish (lira).
292	Emine	(to Göksel)	Talk English, talk English!
293	Göksel		Hey! Make some money for the melons!
294	Banu		We always make pounds, why don't we make pence!
295	Göksel		Make some money for the melons. Twenty p yes. Melons, fifty pounds?
296	Banu		Yeah! There is.
297	Göksel		What's gonna be fifty pounds?
298	Banu		Some money, some money!
299	Emine		Talk English!

Transcript A (Store 1 – Nicosia): 287-299 Banu, Göksel, Emine

Extract 6.1.3

51 Researcher		*Evet ! Karpuzcu geldi.*	Yes! The melon
		Merhaba! Karpuz istermisiniz?	Hello! Would you like some melons?
52 Funda		*Evet, daha alalım.*	Yes, we'll have some more.
53 Researcher		*Kaç tane daha?*	How many more?
54 Binnur		*Yirmi tane.*	Twenty of them.
55 Researcher	(counts in Turkish, children join in the counting)	*Size bir haberim var. Londra'da bir dükkan sizden Karpuz almak istiyor.*	I have some news for you. A store in London wants to buy melons from you.
56 Funda		*Tamam! Satarık gennerine.*	OK! we'll sell them.
			(meaning we will sell *to* them)

Transcript A (Store 1 – Nicosia): 51-56 Funda, Binnur, Researcher

Extract 7.1.2

71 Funda		*Neyse, daha karpuzcu gelecek..*	The melon man has not come yet.
		Tertipleyelim hade gelin.	Let's tidy up.
		Paralarımızı saklayalım.	Let's hide our money.
		Hadeyiniz gelin ne güzel tertipleyelim.	Come on! Let's tidy up really nicely.
		Gelsin yarın o karpuzcu.	I hope he will come tomorrow.
		Ahh. Evimi özledim be.	Ahh! I miss my home.
		Daha gelecek	He still hasn't come yet.
72 Şefik	(being silly)		I want to see my wife!
73 Funda		*Amman be yoruldum.*	Oh! I am tired.
		Uyuyalım.	Let's sleep.
	(to Sefik)	*Gezdiniz.*	You have been around.
74 Şefik		*Daha şimdi...*	Now we just ...
75 Funda		*Hade dustbin'e atalım bunları.*	Come on, let's put these in the dustbin!
76 Şefik		*Ben palavra yaparım!*	I do a lot of nonsense things.
77 Binnur	(to Sefik)	*Sus be!*	Be quiet you!
78 Şefik			What's that around the money?...That's our wages!

Transcript A (Store 1 – Nicosia): 71-78 Şefik, Binnur, Funda

Bibliography

Adalar, N. (1997) 'Borrowed Nouns, Bilingual People: The Case of the Londralıs in Northern Cyprus'. *International Symposium on Bilingualism: Abstracts* Department of Speech, University of Newcastle Upon Tyne.

Alkan, F. and Costantinides, S. (1982) *Cypriots in Haringey*, London: Haringey Borough Council.

Al-Rasheed, M. (1994) 'The Myth of Return: Iraqi Arab and Assyrian refugees in London', *Journal of Refugee Studies*, Vol.7, No.2/3 pp.199-219.

Anthias, F. (1983) 'Sexual Divisions and Ethnic Adaptation: the case of Greek-Cypriot Women.' In Phizacklea, A. (ed.) *One Way Ticket: Migration and Female Labour.* London: Routledge and Kegan Paul.

Badcock, J. (2002) *Terror and Asylum: Turkish Kurds in Britain*, Northposition Online Magazine.

Baker, C. (1988) *Key Issues in Bilingualism and Bilingual Education.* Clevedon: Multilingual Matters.

Baker, C. (1996) (first edition) *Foundation of Bilingual Education and Bilingualism*, Clevedon: Multilingual Matters Ltd.

Baker, C. (2001) (third edition) *Foundation of Bilingual Education and Bilingualism*, Clevedon: Multilingual Matters Ltd.

Ben Zeev, S. (1977) 'The Influence of Bilingualism on Cognitive Strategy and Cognitive Development', *Child Development* 48, p1009-1018.

Berger, J. (1975) *A Seventh Man: A Book of Images and Words about the Experience of Migrant Workers in Europe*, Harmondsworth: Penguin

Bialystok, E. (1991) *Language Processing in Bilingual Children*, Cambridge: Cambridge University Press.

Broughton, J. (1987) *Critical Theories of Psychological Development*, New York: Plenum.

Bruner, J.S. (1972) *The Relevance of Education*, Gil, A. (ed.) London: Allen and Unwin.

Buckingham, D. (1993) *Children Talking Television*, Lewes: Falmer.

Burris, V.L. (1983) 'Stages in the Development of Economic Concepts', in *Human Development*, 36, p.791-812.

Butterworth, E. and Kinnibrugh, D. (1970) *The Social Background of Immigrant Children from India, Pakistan and Cyprus.* Scope Handbook 1.Harlow: Longman/Books for Schools Council, p.69-75.

Centre for Information on Language Teaching and Research CILT (1983) *Turkish: Language Culture Guide*, London: CILT

Clough, H. E. and Quarmby, J. (1978) *A Public Library Service for Ethnic Minorities in Great Britain*, London: CILT.

Collison, P. (1969) 'Immigrants' Varieties of experiences', *New Society*, 26th June and in *Race and Immigration*, New Society Social Studies Reader, p.16-18.

Collinson, S. (1990) Alevi Kurd Asylum Seekers, unpublished M. Phil thesis, Cambridge.

Constantinides, P. (1977) 'The Greek Cypriots: Factors in the Maintenance of Ethnic Identity', in Watson, J.L. (ed.) *Between Two Cultures*, Oxford: Basil Blackwell.

Cummins, J. (1977) 'Cognitive Factors Associated with the Attainment of Intermediate Levels of Bilingual Skills', *Modern Language Journal* 61, 3-12.

Cummins, J. (1980) 'The Construct of Language Proficiency in Bilingual Education' in Alatis, J.E. (ed.) *Georgetown University Round Table on Languages and Linguistics* 1980, Washington, DC: Georgetown University Press.

Danziger, K. (1958). 'Children's Earliest Conceptions of Economic Relationships', *Journal of Social Psychology* (Australia) 47 p.231 -240.

Davies, B. and Banks, C. (1992) 'The Gender Trap: A Feminist- Poststructuralist analysis of Primary School Children's Talk About Gender, *Junior Curriculum Studies*, 24 (1) p.1-25.

Dick, M. (2002) *New Refugees: People from Kurdistan*, Birmingham City Website.

Dirim, I. and Hieronymus, A. (2003) 'Cultural Orientation and Language use among Multilingual Youth Groups': 'For me it is like we all speak one language' in Jorgensen, J. (ed.) *Bilingualism and Social Change*, Clevendon: Multilingual Matters.

Donaldson, M. (1978) *Children's Minds*, Fontana Press: London.

Fishman, J. A. (1991) *Reversing Language Shift*, Cleveland: Multilingual Matters.

Foucault, M. (1980) *Power/Knowledge*, Sussex: Harvester Press.

Francis. B. (1998) *Power Plays: Primary School Children's Constructions of Gender, Power and Adult Work*, Staffordshire: Trentham Books.

Furth, H. (1978) 'Young Children's Understanding of Society', in Mcgurk, H. (ed.) *Issues in Childhood Social Development*, Cambridge: University Press.

Furth, H. (1980) *The World of Grown-ups*, New York: Elsevier.

George, V. and Millerson, G. (1967) ' The Cypriot Community in London', *Race*, VIII, 3, 277-92.

General Register Office Census, (1966) *Great Britain*, London: HMSO.

General Register Office (GRO) (1956) *Census 1951, England and Wales, General Tables*, London: HMSO.

General Register Office (GRO) (1964) *Census 1961, England and Wales, Birthplace and Nationality Tables*. London: HMSO.

George, V. (1960) The Assimilation of the Cypriot Community in London. Unpublished MA thesis, University of Nottingham

George, V. and Millerson, G. (1967) ' The Cypriot Community in London', *Race*, VIII, 3, 277-92.

Goldstein, B. and Oldham, J. (eds.) (1979) *Children and Work*, New Jersey: Transaction Books.

Gordon, P. (1983) 'Back to Cyprus?', *New Society*, 4 August,170-171.

Griffiths, D.J. (2002) *Somali and Kurdish Refugees in London: New Identities in the Diaspora*, Burlington: Ashgate.

Hackney Council, (1993) *Planning for the Turkish/Kurdish Community in Hackney*, Hackney Council, Environmental Services, London.

Haringey Council (1997) *Refugees and Asylum Seekers in Haringey*, Research Project Report, Haringey Council, London.

Holroyd, S. (1990) 'Children's Development in Socio-Economic Ideas: Some Psychological Perspectives', in Ross, A. (ed.) *Economic and Industrial Awareness in the Primary School*, London: PNL/SCIP.

Hong Kwang, R. and Stacey, B. (1977) The Understanding of Socio-Economic Concepts in Malaysian Chinese School Children, *Child Study Journal* 11 p.33-49.

Hutchings, M. (1990) 'Children's Thinking About work' in Ross, A. (ed.) *Economic and Industrial Awareness in the Primary School*, London: PNL press /SCIP.

Issa, T. (1987) Bilingual Education of Turkish Speaking Children in a Multicultural Environment, unpublished MSc thesis, London: Polytechnic of the South Bank.

Issa, T. (1993) 'Language Choice in Bilingual Turkish/English Primary School Children', a Comparative Survey, London.

Issa, T. (2002) Augmentation of Language and Thinking in Bilingual Children, Unpublished PhD Thesis, University of North London.

Issa, T. (2004b) 'Yok Bir Grandfathers' Clock': The Attitudes and Uses of Cypriot Turkish in the British Context, in *International Journal of Sociolinguistics*, Dec.2004.

Izady, M.R (1992) *The Kurds: A Concise Handbook*. London: Taylor and Francis.

Jahoda. G. (1979) 'The Construction of Economic Reality by Some Glaswegian Children, *European Journal of Social Psychology*, 19 p.115-127.

Jahoda, G. (1983) 'European Lag in the Development of an Economic Concept: a Study in Zimbabwe', *British Journal of Developmental Psychology* 1 p.110-123.

Kardash, C. A. *et al.* (1988) Bilingual Referents in Cognitive Processing, *Contemporary Educational Psychology* 13, p.45-57.

Karmiloff-Smith, A. (1992) *Beyond Modularity: A Developmental Perspective on Cognitive Science*, Cambridge, MA: MIT Press.

Kourilisky, M.L. and Graff, E. (1985) Children's Use of Cost Benefit Analysis: Developmental or Non-existent, Paper Presented at the Annual Meeting of the American Educational Research Association: Chicago.

Kreyenbroek, P. G. (1992) 'On the Kurdish Language' in Kreyenbroek, P.G and Sperl, S. (eds.) *The Kurds: a contemporary overview*, Routledge, London.

Ladbury, S. (1977) 'The Turkish Cypriots: Ethnic Relations in London and Cyprus', in Watson, J.L (ed.) *Between Two Cultures: Migrants and Minorities in Britain*, Oxford: Basil Blackwell.

Laiser, S. (1996) *Martyrs, Traitors and Patriots: Kurdistan after the Gulf War*, London: Zed Books.

Lipman, M. (1988) *Thinking in Education*, Cambridge: Cambridge University Press.

Lloyd, B. and Duveen, G. (1992) *Gender Identities and Education*, London: Harvester.

London Council of Social Service (LCSS) (1967) *Commonwealth Children in Britain*, London: National Council of Social Service.

Luria, A.R. (1973) *The Working Brain*, Baltimore, Maryland: Penguin.

Marcuse, P. (1996) 'Of Walls and Immigrant Enclaves', in Baubock, R. and Zolberg, A. (eds.) *The Challenge of Diversity: Integration and Pluralism in Societies of Immigration*, London: Avebury.

McDowall, D. (1989) *The Kurds*, Minority Rights Group, London.

Mehmet Ali, A. (1991) 'The Turkish speech Community' in Alladina, S. and Edwards, V. (eds.) *Multilingualism in the British Isles*, London and New York: Longman

Mehmet Ali, A. (2001) *Turkish Speaking Communities and Education: No Delight*, London: Fatal Publications.

Memdouh, M. (1981) *The Report of the Cyprus Turkish Association on the Educational Needs of the Turkish community in London and in England*, London: Cyprus Turkish Association.

Middleton, P. (1992) *The Inward Gaze: Masculinity and Subjectivity in Modern Culture*, London: Routledge.

Oakley, R. (1968) 'The Cypriot Background' in Oakley, R. (ed) *New Backgrounds: the Immigrant Child at Home and School*. Oxford: Oxford University Press.

Oakley, R. (1970) 'The Cypriots in Britain', *Race Today* p.99-102.

Oakley, R. (1971) Cypriot Migration and Settlement in Britain, Unpublished D.Phil. Thesis, University of Oxford.

Oakley, R. (1979) 'Family Kinship and Patronage: the Cypriot Migration to Britain' in Khan, S. (ed) *Minority Families in Britain: Support and Stress*. London: Macmillan.

Office of Population Censuses and Surveys (OPCS) (1995) *International Passenger Survey*, London: HMSO.

Office of Population and Censuses and Surveys (OPCS) (1974) *Census 1971, Great Britain, Country of Birth Tables*, London: HMSO.

Office of Population and Censuses and Surveys (OPCS) (1975) *International Migration: Citizenship, 1964 to 1974.* London HMSO.

Paine, S. (1974) Exporting Workers, the Turkish Case, *Occasional Paper* 41, Cambridge: Cambridge University Press.

Refugee Council, (2000) *Helping Refugee Children in Schools,* London: Refugee Council.

Reid, E., Smith, G. and Morawska, A. (1985) *Languages in London: CLE/LMP Working Paper,* No.12, London: Community Languages and Education Project, University of London Institute of Education

Reilly, R. (1991) Political Identity, Protest and Power amongst Kurdish Refugees in Britain, unpublished MA thesis Cambridge University, Churchill College.

Ricciardelli, L.A. (1992) Creativity and Bilingualism, *Journal of Creative Behaviour* 26 (4) p.242-254.

Richman, N. (1995) They Don't Recognise Our Dignity: A Study of Young Refugees in the London Borough Of Hackney, Unpublished research, City and Hackney NHS Trust.

Ross, A. (1990) 'Economic and Industrial Awareness and the Primary School Child', in Ross, A. (ed.) *Economic and Industrial Awareness in the Primary School,* London: PNL/SCIP.

Ross, A. (1992) 'Children's Perceptions of Capital' in Hutchings, M. and Wade, W. (eds.) *Developing Economic and Industrial Understanding in the Primary School,* London: PNL Press.

Ross, A. (2003) 'Cultures, Identity and Education in Europe' in Ross, A. (ed.) A Europe of Many Cultures, Proceedings of the fifth conference of the Children's Identity and Citizenship in Europe Thematic Network, Braga 2003. London CICE Publication.

Rutter, J. (1994) *Refugee Children in the Classroom.* Stoke on Trent: Trentham Books.

Rutter, J. (2003) (second edition) *Supporting Refugee Children in the 21st Century: A compendium of Essential Information,* Stoke on Trent: Trentham Books.

Ransdell, S.E. and Fisher, I. (1989) 'Effects of Concreteness and Tasks Context on Recall of Prose Among Bilingual and Monolingual Speakers', *Journal of Memory and Language* 26, p.392-405.

Ryan, N. (1995) 'Television Nation', *Wired,* March 1997, p.4-10.

Saraçoğlu, E. (1992) *Kıbrıs Ağzı.* Lefkosa: Türk Tarih Kurumu Basimevi

Saran, R. and Neisser, B. (eds.) (2004) *Enquiring Minds – Socratic Dialogue in Education,* Stoke on Trent: Trentham Books

Stubbs, M. (ed.) (1985) *The Other Languages of England: Linguistic Minorities Project.* London: Routledge.

Schug, M. and Birkley, C. (1985) 'The Development of Children's Economic Reasoning', *Theory And Research in Social Education,* 13 p.31-42.

Strauss, A. (1952) 'The Development and Transformation of Monetary Meanings in The Child', *American Sociological Review* 17 p.275-284.

Sutton, R. (1962) Behaviour in the Attainment of Economic Concepts, *Journal of Psychology* 53 p.37-46.

Tan, H. and Stacey, B. (1981) The Understanding of Socio-Economic Concepts in Malaysian Chinese School Children, *Child Study Journal* 21 p.33-49.

Taylor, M. J. (1988) *Worlds Apart?* NFER-Nelson.

Triseliotis, J.P. (1976) 'Immigrants of Mediterranean Origin' *Child Care, Health and Development,* 2, 395-378.

Turner V.W. (1957) *Schism and Continuity in an African Society: A study of Ndembu village Life,* Manchester University Press for the Rhodes-Livingstone Institute, Manchester.

Ulug, F. (1981) A study of conflicting cultural pressures with particular attention to the Turkish Cypriot community and a small group of secondary school Turkish girls living in North London, Unpublished H.Ed. dissertation, Middlesex Polytechnic.

United Kingdom, Parliament, House of Commons, (1985) *Education for All: Final Report of the Committee of Inquiry Into the Education of Children from Ethnic Minority Groups.* London: HMSO.

van Bruinessen, M. (1992) 'Kurdish Society, Ethnicity, Nationalism and Refugee Problems' in Kreyenbroek, P.G and Sperl, S. (eds) *The Kurds: A Contemporary Overview.* London: Routledge,

van Bruinessen, M. (1996) 'Diversity and Division Among the Kurds', *War Report: bulletin of the Institute for War and Peace Reporting*, Nov-Dec. 1996, No.47, pp 29-32.

Vygotsky, L.S. (1962) *Thought and Language*, Cambridge, MA: MIT Press.

Vygotsky, L.S. (1978) *Mind in Society: The Development of Higher Psychological Processes*, Cambridge: Harvard University Press.

Wahlbeck, Ö. (1997) 'The Kurdish Diaspora and Refugee Associations in Finland and England' in *Exclusion and Inclusion of Refugees in Contemporary Europe*, Ercomer: University of Utrecht.

Warner, R. (1991) *Dengan Ji Kurdistane, Voices From Kurdistan*, London: Minority Rights Group.

World University Service (1977) *Education for Refugees*, London:WUS.

Yuval-Davis, N. (1997) *Gender and Nation*, London: Sage.

Index